N
DAGG SOUND
DOUBTFUL SOUND
THOMPSON SOUND
NANCY SOUND
CHARLES SOUND
CASWELL SOUND
GEORGE SOUND
BLIGH SOUND
SUTHERLAND SOUND
MILFORD SOUND
Febrero Point
Secretary Island
Deas Cove
Bauza I.
Marble Mine
Gold Arm
Emelius Arm
Poison Bay
Malaspina Reach
Crooked Arm
Bradshaw Sound
Stillwater R.
Anchorage Cove
Escape Cove
Vancouver Arm
L. Marchant
Saddle Hill
L. Alice
L. Katherine
Wild Natives R.
L. Grave
Light R.
Irene R.
Doughton Arm
Coronation Peak
L. Mackinnon
Mt Irene
Henry Pass
Oilskin Pass
Dark R.
Sutherland Falls
Mitre Peak
Hall Arm
Commander Peak
Deep Cove
L. Thomson
Worsley Pass
Hunter Pass
Arthur R.
Mackinnon Pass
Milford Sound
Wilmot Pass
Mt Pisgah
L. Hankinson
Centre Pass
Worsley R.
Power Station
MILFORD TRACK
Homer Tunnel
Middle Fiord
North Fiord
Glade House
South Fiord
Mt Christina
Hollyford R.
LAKE MANAPOURI
LAKE TE ANAU
KEPLER TRACK
Borland Saddle
Waiau R.
Milford Road
Park boundary
MANAPOURI
TE ANAU
Borland Lodge
Waiau R.
LEGEND
Fiordland National Park boundary
Roads
Tracks

The FJORDS of FIORDLAND

Steamer passing the entrance of Doubtful Sound, 1890. Watercolour by L. W. Wilson. *(Courtesy D. Moir)*

The FJORDS of FIORDLAND

John Hall-Jones

Dedication

To the sailors, sealers and whalers
who first explored these fjords

Published by Craig Printing Company Limited,
PO Box 99, Invercargill, New Zealand.

ISBN 0-908629-56-7

Printed by Craig Printing Company Limited, Invercargill, New Zealand.
Email: sales@craigsatlas.co.nz Website: www.craigprint.co.nz
2002-54170

Contents

Also by John Hall-Jones:

Early Fiordland, 1968
Mr Surveyor Thomson, 1971
The Invercargill Rotary Club, 1974, 1999
Bluff Harbour, 1976
Fiordland Explored, 1976
The Invercargill Club, 1979
Fiordland Place Names, 1979
The South Explored, 1979
An Early Surveyor in Singapore, 1980
New Zealand's Majestic Wilderness, 1981
Goldfields of the South, 1982
Pioneers of Te Anau, 1983
The Thomson Paintings of the Straits Settlements, 1983
Glimpses into Life in Malayan Lands, 1984
Doubtfull Harbour, 1984
The Catlins Guidebook, 1985
Jonathan White's New Zealand, 1986
Martins Bay, 1987
Supplement to Doubtfull Harbour, 1988
Footsteps in the Wilderness, 1989
Discover the South, 1991
John Turnbull Thomson: First Surveyor-General, 1992
Stewart Island Explored, 1994
The Horsburgh Lighthouse, 1995
Discover Fiordland, 1997
Milford Sound, 2000

Introduction and Acknowledgements

The appearance of this iron-bound coast cleft asunder into harbours presents a scene truly grand and solitary.
Commander George Richards, 1851

Tucked away in the remote south-west corner of New Zealand is some of the most spectacular scenery on this planet. The steep glacier-carved fjords of Fiordland National Park have won world renown for their grandeur and magnificence. Majestic Milford Sound has been described as the "Eighth Wonder of the World". But Milford Sound is just one of the fourteen fjords that invade the great seawall of Fiordland. Some penetrate much deeper into the forested mountain heartland than Milford and others branch into arms that almost link with each other. Dusky and Doubtful Sounds and Preservation Inlet are so large that they are really inland seas and all three are decked with wooded islands. The splendour of Hall Arm in Doubtful Sound is equal to the majesty of Milford and all the other fjords have special scenic features of their own

"The appearance of this iron-bound coast, cleft asunder as it were into harbours by some awful convulsion of nature, presents a scene truly grand and solitary." So wrote Commander George Richards on the first complete survey of the Fiordland coast by *HMS Acheron* in 1851. "The only natural harbours along the whole West Coast [of the South Island] are those truly remarkable sounds or inlets which penetrate its south-west shores. Approaching from seaward the smaller inlets have more the appearance of ravines between high rugged mountains than entrances of harbours."

From a peak on the south side of Caswell Sound, Commander Richards describes the scene from above. "A view of the surrounding country is perhaps one of the most grand and magnificent spectacles it is possible to imagine. We could only compare the scene around us as far as the eye could reach, to a vast sea of mountains of every possible variety of shape and ruggedness. The clouds and mist floated beneath us, and the harbour appeared no more than an insignificant stream."

Fortuitously this beautiful land of fjords was set aside as a national park in 1904 and Commander Richards' description (of 1851) still holds true today. For this illustrated history of the fjords of Fiordland, they are taken chronologically starting with Captain Cook's "Dusky Bay" and "Doubtfull Harbour". But for those who would like the names of the fjords in order there is an old jingle that gives their sequence starting from Preservation Inlet in the south:–

Preserve your Chalk
It's Dusky in Breaksea
And Dagg says it's Doubtful
If Thompson went round
But Nancy and Charles go to
Caswell for marble
And George and Bligh to see
Sutherland in Milford Sound

The first European to see this wild west coast was the great navigator, James Cook, who sailed the *Endeavour* up the Fiordland coast in 1770. 'Dusk' was gathering as he lay off the entrance of "Dusky Bay" and he decided it would be most unwise to enter this unknown fjord with so many islands lying inside. He continued on to "Doubtfull Harbour", but a large island almost blocked its entrance and he was 'doubtfull' if there would be enough wind inside to sail the *Endeavour* out again.

Three years later Cook was back and this time he entered "Dusky Bay" in the *Resolution* to rest his men and restock with food. During his six weeks sojourn in "Dusky Bay" Cook surveyed the whole fjord to produce an excellent chart of this large and complex waterway. The stumps of the trees that he felled for his observatory on Astronomer Point can still be seen there.

With the publication of Cook's detailed chart of "Dusky Bay" sealers were attracted to this coast and so we find New Zealand's first European houses, the first shipbuilding and the first shipwreck, all in the remote wilds of Dusky Sound. After the shipwreck, there were 244 Europeans living in the fjord, which was more than the total European population of New Zealand at that time and in a place where no-one lives today. Thanks to the recent archaeological investigations of Dr Ian Smith, Karl Gillies and their team, we now know much more about these goings on than we did in the past.

Preservation Inlet was once the scene of two Maori battles, the first whaling station in New Zealand and in the 1890s a major gold rush. With the discovery of gold, two gold towns, Cromarty and Te Oneroa, sprang up on the shores of the inlet to serve the mines and quartz crushing batteries in the hills behind. The impressive remains of these huge crushing batteries can still be seen at Preservation Inlet; also the spectacular reclining chimney of the Tarawera smelter.

Here then, are some of the stories in *The Fjords of Fiordland*. The text includes liberal quotations from the journals of the first Europeans to see the fjords:

- Captain Cook and his officers;
- the Spanish explorers of "Doubtfull Harbour";
- the sealers Robert Murry and John Boultbee;
- Commander Richards and George Hansard of the *Acheron* survey;
- the geologist Sir James Hector;
- the overland explorer William Grave;
- and the delightful pithy phrases of Richard Henry, the "Caretaker of Resolution Island" and discoverer of "a very passable route" to George Sound.

In this illustrated history there are 338 photographs, maps, sketches and early paintings, the majority of which are in colour. Because of their vintage, most of the historical pictures are in black and white, but historic sites have been photographed in colour. Colour has also been used extensively to illustrate the sheer beauty of this wilderness of fjords. The secret of photographing in Fiordland, with all its changing moods, is to be in the right place at the right time. You can revisit one particular spot a dozen times before striking the right day when the sunlight is perfect and the sea is calm with mirror reflections.

This book would not have been possible without the help of a number of special friends who have accompanied me on expeditions to the fjords over the years and who have generously made their photographs available. Alistair Carey and Tom Couzens, my two mates on the Canterbury Museum expeditions that explored and mapped the unknown hinterland of Charles Sound in the early 1950s. Later, with Brian Reid we discovered a kakapo track and bowl system in George Sound. Leigh Morris and Russell Wall, who suffered five foodless days with me in North Port at Cape Providence. My 'BT' (Big Trip) mate Bruce Miles. I first teamed up with Bruce on an expedition to Preservation Inlet in 1976 and over the next 15 years we traversed the hinterland of the fjords in a series of great sweeping tramps which became known as our annual 'BTs'.

During the past four years my German friend Dieter Kraft and I have been exploring the fjords by sea-kayak, which is a superb way of getting close to nature and offers wonderful opportunities for photographs. In our annual kayaking expeditions to the fjords we have worked our way systematically round Doubtful Sound, Dusky Sound, Preservation Inlet and in 2001 we undertook a 'Triple Sounds' expedition to Sutherland, Bligh and Charles Sounds. Neither of us will ever forget our paddle out into the Tasman Sea from Sutherland Sound and down to Bligh Sound, as fast as our paddles could paddle!

I am indebted to the Department of Conservation (DOC) for a number of trips on its patrol vessel *Renown* (skippers John Ward, Lance Shaw and Bob Walker) surveying historic sites in the fjords, which provided unique opportunities to explore and photograph these remote and inaccessible places. For the past nine years I have enjoyed working as a lecturer-guide on the *Milford Wanderer* (skippers Maru Bradshaw and Peter Bloxham) on winter cruises to Doubtful and Dusky Sounds, Preservation and Chalky Inlets, which has furthered my chances to explore and photograph. Likewise I am grateful to Lance Shaw for a trip in his yacht *Breaksea Girl* to the northern fjords and for sharing his special knowledge of the coastline with me. Bill Gibson and Daphne Taylor of Fiordland Wilderness Experiences for the hire of the their sea-kayak with which we explored the fjords. Commander Larry Robbins of *HMNZS Monowai* for an unforgettable ten days with the Navy while surveying Preservation and Chalky Inlets.

I wish to thank Reva Calvert for providing me with her excellent history of Tarewai's greenstone mere and for allowing me to photograph this famous patu. The Department of Conservation (DOC), the Hocken Library, the Alexander Turnbull Library and the Invercargill Public Library have assisted me considerably with the illustrations. Also institutions overseas – the British Maritime Museum, the British Admiralty and the Museo Naval in Spain.

I wish to thank my publishers, Craig Printing Company Limited, for all their care and attention in producing such a handsome, well designed book.

Finally I am most grateful to my wife, Pamela, for checking through this manuscript so thoroughly for me.

CHAPTER 1

Sounds or Fjords?

Sounds and fjords are both inlets of the sea, but a sound is formed by a river and a fjord is carved by a glacier.
From the Oxford Dictionary

It is an interesting point that although there are fourteen deep, glacier-carved fjords on the West Coast of Fiordland not one of them goes by the name of fjord, they are all called 'sounds'. Bearing in mind the definition of a fjord, a glacier-carved inlet of the **sea,** they should all be called fjords. It was the early sealers from Great Britain and Australia who, being familiar with the river-formed sounds of their homelands, named the inlets of the West Coast 'sounds' instead of fjords. As is the way with fishermen and sealers their names for the 'sounds' often became abbreviated, so that George Sound became George's, Bligh Sound Bligh's, Nancy Sound Nancy's and so on. Many of the original names were given by the famous Welsh sealer Captain John Grono and are recorded on an early map of the West Coast Fjords by the French sealer Edward Meurant c.1826.

Captain John Lort Stokes, in the first complete survey of the West Coast Fjords in *HMS Acheron* in 1851, had a heaven-sent opportunity to correct the terminology from sound to fjord. Unfortunately he opted for the former and the fjords became known as the West Coast Sounds.

Conversely, long after the West Coast Sounds were named, the name 'fjord' appeared on the map of Lake Te Anau. Captain Edward Hankinson RN of Lynwood Station had taken part in the search for Sir John Franklin when he went missing in the Arctic. The long, narrow, steep-walled arms of Lake Te Anau reminded Captain Hankinson of the fjords of Greenland and, after carrying out some charting of Lake Te Anau, he gave the name fiord to the three main arms of the lake – South Fiord, Middle Fiord and North Fiord. Captain Hankinson passed on the result of his charting and naming to surveyor James McKerrow and McKerrow perpetuated the names of the three fiords on his map of Lake Te Anau in 1863.

Strictly speaking the three fiords of Lake Te Anau, although glacier-sculptured, are not true fjords because they are the arms of a lake and not the sea. Nevertheless, thanks to this use of the term fiord at Lake Te Anau, the name became established on the map and the whole region became known as

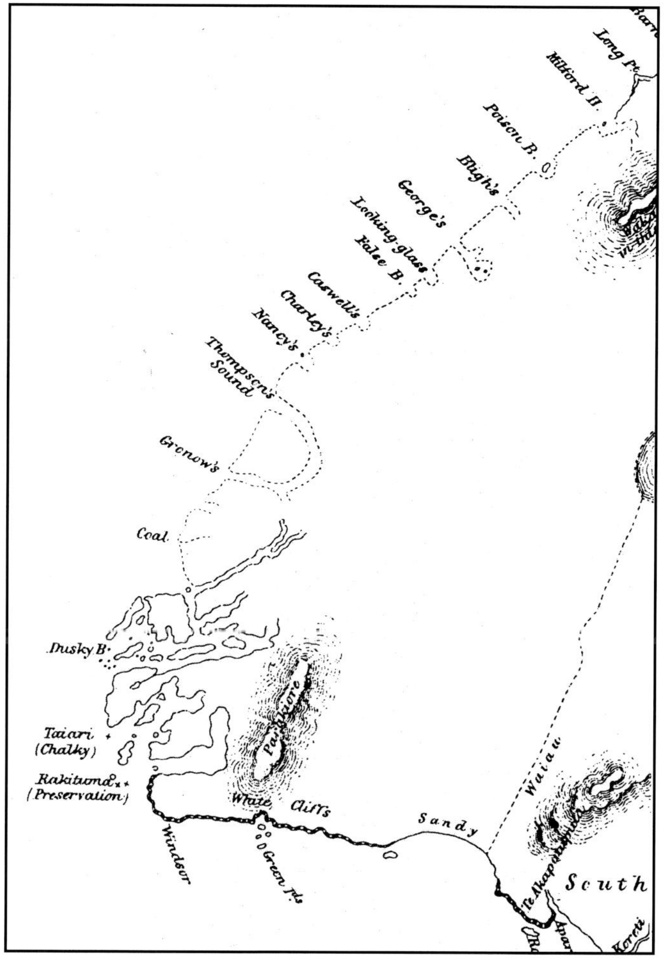

Edward Meurant's map of the West Coast Fjords, c.1826, giving the early sealers' names for the fjords. Note Milford H. (Haven) and "Gronow's" for Doubtful Sound. *(E. Shortland)*

Morning mist hangs above the South Fiord of Lake Te Anau where a large glacier once flowed. *(J. Hall-Jones)*

Captain Edward Hankinson R.N. who gave the name fiord to the three main arms of Lake Te Anau. *(G. A. Hamilton)*

Fiord County and eventually as Fiordland National Park.

For the above reasons the term fjord is used instead of sound in the text when speaking generally of the West Coast Sounds. Likewise the spelling fjord is preferred to fiord, being the correct Norwegian spelling of the name which originated from the fjords of Norway.

Geologically Speaking

The fourteen majestic fjords that we see today are the end result of erosion by glaciers over the last two million years, the last great ice age taking place from 80,000 to 10,000 years ago. Glaciers in the west flowed down to the ocean gouging out troughs well below sea level and dumping the debris at their mouths. When the ice melted the sea flooded in forming deep inner basins and shallower entrances, often with islands, where the glacier debris had been deposited.

The oldest fjords are in the far south, Preservation and Chalky Inlets, where the land flattens out noticeably, tapering down to the ocean. The two inlets and their neighbour, Dusky Sound, have much wider, shallower entrances than their northern counterparts and are studded with islands, reefs and

submerged rocks, the leftovers of their glacier deposits. These southernmost fjords, including Doubtful Sound, are also more complex having extensive branching waterways. The longest of the fjords, Dusky Sound, extends 44 kilometres inland and the second longest, Doubtful Sound, 40 kilometres inland.

The fjords north of Doubtful Sound tend to be simpler, non-branching and higher-walled. They culminate in Milford Sound, the youngest of them all, where the sea-cliffs soar straight from the water's edge and the last of the once proud Milford Glacier can be seen as icefields on the summits of Mts Pembroke and Tutoko.

Top left: Mist outlines the succession of glacier-carved fjords and valleys of the West Coast, where large glaciers once flowed down to the sea. Looking south along the coast from the entrance of Bligh Sound. *(DOC)*

Left: Soft clouds fill the South Fiord, a likeness to the large glacier that carved out this arm of Lake Te Anau. *(J. Hall-Jones)*

CHAPTER 2

Historic Dusky Sound

Five high peaked rocks standing up like the four fingers and thum of a Man's hand.
James Cook, 1770

Painting of the entrance to "Dusky Bay" by William Hodges, 1773. *(Mitchell Library)*

As James Cook sailed the barque *Endeavour* up the Fiordland coast in 1770 he spotted the jagged pinnacles of Five Fingers Point "standing up like the four fingers and thum of a Man's hand" at the entrance to "Dusky Bay". But 'dusk' was gathering and the prudent Cook decided that it would be most unwise to sail the *Endeavour* into this unknown, uncharted fjord with its many islands and submerged rocks.

Three years later, after four months sailing among the icebergs of the Antarctic, Cook headed north to "Dusky Bay" in the barque *Resolution* to rest his men and restock the ship's larder. This time it was almost midday as he approached the mouth of "Dusky Bay" on 26 March 1773 and he sailed the *Resolution* straight inside to anchor off Anchor Point, at the innermost tip of Anchor Island. The green wooded islands of the fjord contrasted strangely with

Five Fingers Point, "standing up like the four fingers and thum of a Man's hand". *(J. Hall-Jones)*

"The Narrows", Cook's passage into Pickersgill Harbour, was only twice the width of the ship. Photographed from Astronomer Point. *(J. Hall-Jones)*

Astronomer Point

The base for their activities in "Dusky Bay" for the next five weeks is illustrated beautifully in a painting by the artist William Hodges. The barque *Resolution* is shown close into Astronomer Point where "her yards were locked among the branches". A rata tree growing horizontally across

Below: Pickersgill Harbour, showing the route of the *Resolution* through "The Narrows". Also the observatory on "Astronymers Point" and the tents at the "Watering Place" (Cook Stream). *(British Museum)*

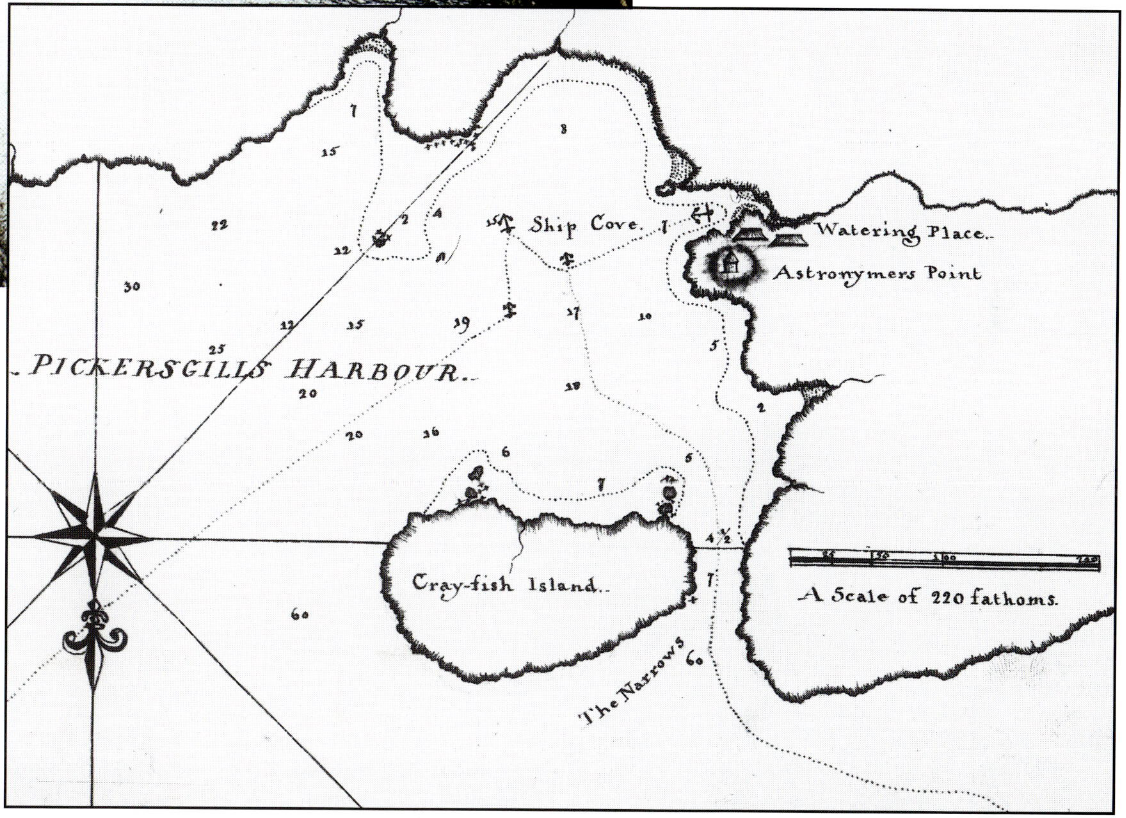

the bare, white icebergs of the Antarctic. "Flocks of aquatic birds enlivened the rocky shores and the whole country resounded with the wild notes of the feathered tribe."

But Anchor Point is exposed to all the whims of the prevailing winds in Dusky and Lieutenant Richard Pickersgill, who Cook describes as "a good officer, but liking ye grog", was sent to search for a safer anchorage. Pickersgill reported on a "snug little harbour" on the south side of the fjord and on 27 March Cook worked the *Resolution* over to Pickersgill Harbour, passing through a narrow passage, The Narrows, "scarcely twice the width of the ship", to moor alongside Astronomer Point.

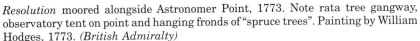

Resolution moored alongside Astronomer Point, 1773. Note rata tree gangway, observatory tent on point and hanging fronds of "spruce trees". Painting by William Hodges, 1773. *(British Admiralty)*

Endeavour replica in the same position in 1996. *(J. Hall-Jones)*

the water served as a gangway and a seaman is seen making his way back to the ship. Up on the crest of the point the astronomer, William Wales, has erected his observatory tent to fix the latitude and the longitude of Astronomer Point. Nearby someone has hung out the washing to dry. Easily recognisable in the painting are the hanging fronds of two rimu ("spruce") trees, an essential ingredient of the "spruce beer" that they brewed onshore.

As depicted correctly by the artist, the gangway was quite a substantial affair, a second tree being felled and laid on the gunnel alongside the living rata tree. Then cross pieces and planking laid on top, with a handrail leading off from the bank.

In 1996 Captain Chris Blake manoeuvred the *Endeavour* replica into the same position as her sister ship back in 1773, a truly moving sight. Whereas it is nice to think that the horizontal rata shown in the photograph was the original gangway, it is more likely to have been another rata log, now in the sea near the present landing for the Astronomer Point board walk.

Also at this landing there is a very old cut rata branch overhanging the sea which could well have been the same branch from which William Wales suspended his tide gauge tube to measure the change in tide levels. To his astonishment his tide tube showed that the tides in the fjord fluctuated by a remarkable "8 feet".

To obtain an uninterrupted view for his observations William Wales felled almost an acre of bush on the top of Astronomer Point, "cutting down and destroying more trees and curious shrubs and plants that would in London have sold for one hundred pounds". Levelling the ground for his observatory

he filled a "puncheon of stones and gravel" as a solid stand for the quadrant. Finding the ground still too soft and unsteady he mounted the quadrant and also the clock (Kendall's clock to measure longitude) on two tree stumps close beside each other. Wales was now able to proceed with his work of fixing the position of Astronomer Point. In spite of the "almost continual clowded sky" Wales was able to ascertain the latitude and longitude of his observatory with a remarkable degree of accuracy. When checked by the Navy hydrographers in 1995 (their figures are given in brackets) using all the modern day instruments at their disposal, they were highly impressed to find that his latitude of 45°47'27" South (45°47'43" South) was virtually correct and that his longitude of 166°18'9" East (166°34'26" East) was only slightly out. A truly remarkable result, particularly as longitude was notoriously difficult to measure in those days.

Also on the brow of the point was the forge and anvil which "resounded with the strokes of the hammer". Here too was a "green hut for the woodcutters" and a pen for the sheep they had brought with them.

Cut rata branch at Astronomer Point landing, perhaps the one where William Wales mounted his tide tube. *(J. Hall-Jones)*

Left: Photograph of Wales' tree stumps on Astronomer Point in 1905, perhaps the pair where he mounted the quadrant and clock. *(R. Duncan)*

Secluded Lake Forster at the head of Cook Creek, where the Forsters caught a giant kokupu. *(J. Hall-Jones)*

Spruce Beer

About 100 metres astern of the *Resolution* was a fine freshwater stream (now called Cook Stream) with a wide rocky shelf at its mouth, where there was "another animated scene of business". Here were tents for the sailmakers to mend the sails, a workshop for the coopers to repair the water casks and a small brewery, the first brewery in New Zealand, to brew Cook's "spruce" beer. The latter was concocted by boiling "spruce" (rimu) and "tea tree" (manuka) leaves, adding molasses and wort juice, then fermenting the mixture with yeast. Cook, who insisted on everyone drinking the product as a preventative against scurvy, describes it encouragingly as a "very good well tasted beer", but the crew thought otherwise and pronounced it as foul. The Swedish botanist, Anders Sparrman, reveals how they overcame the problem. "After a small amount of rum and brown sugar had been added and stirred in, it bubbled and tasted rather like champagne".

The ship's two naturalists, the Germans Johann Forster and his son George, and Anders Sparrman, waded up Cook Stream to discover secluded Lake Forster. "Here was the deepest silence", writes Sparrman, "and nature was hushed; not a breath of wind penetrated to this sheet of water enclosed by high hills and great forests; not a single fly or insect, much less a bird, was seen or heard. Only a quite small but new and scaleless pike (the giant kokupu, *Galaxias argenteus*), patterned as though by hieroglyphics, was caught and made a pleasing reward for our trouble."

Ascent of Mt Sparrman

On 23 April Anders Sparrman, Pickersgill and the master, Joseph Gilbert, climbed up alongside the magnificent waterfall at Cascade Cove to reach the top of Mt Sparrman and be rewarded with a superb panoramic view. "We

Rock shelf at the mouth of Cook Stream, the site of New Zealand's first brewery. Rata 'gangway' in background. *(J. Hall-Jones)*

Sparrman ascending Cascade Falls to climb Mt Sparrman. *(A. Sparrman)*

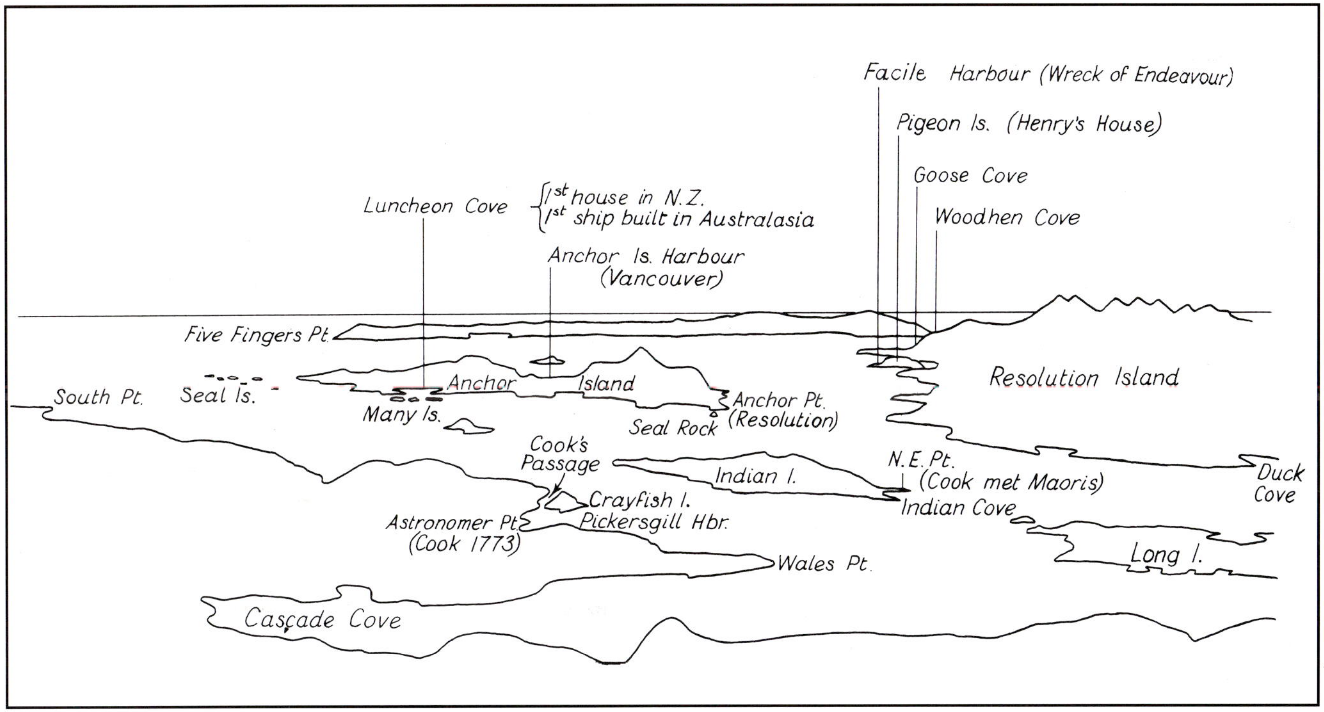

Above right: The view of the entrance to Dusky Sound from Mt Sparrman. Painting by John Buchanan, 1863. *(Buchanan papers)*

Right: Outline of Buchanan's painting to show the historic sites of Dusky Sound. *(Copyright J. Hall-Jones)*

Hodges' painting of the Maori family standing at the foot of one of the cascades of Cascade Falls. *(British Admiralty)*

entrance to Dusky Sound.) "To mark our successful climb", writes Sparrman, "we set fire to the [snowgrass which rapidly took hold] providing the most beautiful illumination to watch from the ship in the evening." A suitable way to celebrate St George's Day, as it happened to be. "The descent from the mountain was much quicker, but much more dangerous. Sometimes perilous ravines barred our way and often we dragged down fair-sized trees whose roots were not firm."

"The waterfall cascaded down in separate falls with a fury and a roar that drowned all voices and sounds in the vicinity. Beams of light formed beautiful rainbow arches in the ascending mists from the torrents of water. Underneath were great heaps of rocks piled up by the power and violence of the stream making, as it were, a great dam in the water." (225 years later, on 23 April 1998, a group of enthusiastic climbers repeated the ascent, albeit on a miserably wet day, to celebrate this first serious climb by Europeans in New Zealand.)

William Hodges visited the waterfall to paint a Maori family standing on one of these "dams" at the foot of one of Sparrman's cascades. Whereas previously it was thought to have been an inaccurate painting of the base of the waterfall, where it becomes a stream to enter the sea, it is now realised that it is a remarkably true depiction of the fall where it exits from a keyhole crevice some 100 metres above sea-level. Likewise, another waterfall painting by Hodges, once thought to be the Cascade Falls

enjoyed an extensive view of the sea [to the west]", records Sparrman, "and to the southward we could see the rest of the great snowclad mountains of the interior, dangerously steep precipices and forest clad valleys. [Below lay] the many islets of Dusky Bay, islands and holms." (Years later in 1863 another botanist, John Buchanan repeated the climb and painted this view of the

The same cascade exiting from its keyhole crevice. *(J. Hall-Jones)*

Above right: Hodges' painting of the waterfall in Nine Fathoms Passage. Cooper Island on left, Mt Solitary in background. *(British Maritime Museum)*

Below right: The same view, with snow on the summit of Mt Solitary. *(J. Hall-Jones)*

using a lot of artistic licence, has now been identified as a fine painting of the waterfall in Nine Fathoms Passage in Cook Channel.

Exploring Dusky Bay

The young Sparrman, he was only 24, enjoyed these expeditions away from the ship exploring and charting the fjord and foraging for food. "Now and then the gun was aimed at some flying seabird or diving penguin. During some hasty pause to take soundings the botanists hurried [ashore] to pick a few flowers or shoot some new bird. Before night came we were busy pitching camp on some sandy or pebbly shore. A number of oars, propped against a tree and covered with the sail, served as a tent. With the assistance of tarred oakum, sprinkled with a little gun powder, the sailors got a fire going to dry out their clothes. Fish and birds were soon roasting on the embers and kegs of spruce beer were summoned to quench the thirst. All this time we were entertained at the fireside by some amusing comedy or some coarse sally or wit. Finally we

Hodges' sketch of the Maori family on Indian Point, 1773. *(Alexander Turnbull Library)*

enjoyed a sweet but short slumber on a bedding of twigs or ferns, where we lay wrapped in our cloaks."

Cook landed in secluded Indian Cove on Indian Island to make his first contact with a Maori family on the rocky north-east point of the island, immediately above the cove. While Cook presented the family with gifts of beads, trinkets and medals, William Hodges sketched the group. (In 1825 the sealer John Boultbee landed at Indian Point and "found one of Cook's medals amongst a heap of rubbish. I foolishly gave it away for a trifle", he writes in his journal, but he leaves us a sketch of both sides of the medal.)

Many years later, Richard Henry also visited the point excavating one of the 'ovens' of the "pit-dwellers", as he called them. Two of these 'ovens' are still obvious on Indian Point and being over knee-deep it is more likely that they were storage pits than ovens.

While surveying around Anchor Island Cook visited a "very snug cove sheltered from all winds, which we called Luncheon Cove, because here we

The same view (as at left). Tip of Long Island on right, Resolution Island on left. *(J. Hall-Jones)*

Secluded Indian Cove at Indian Point. *(J. Hall-Jones)*

One of the pits of the "pit-dwellers" on Indian Point, 1999. *(J. Hall-Jones)*

dinned on crawfish on the side of a pleasant brook shaded by the trees from both wind and sun". After luncheon they rowed out to the outermost islands (Seal Islands) where they saw many seals, slaughtering fourteen for food, which they found "little inferior to beefsteaks".

Proceeding to Goose Cove, Cook rescued a party of duck-shooters who had been stranded after their boat had broken adrift on the falling tide. Here Cook liberated five geese that he had picked up at the Cape of Good Hope. But when one of his young midshipmen, George Vancouver, checked there 18 years later as commander of his own expedition, he found no

Goose Cove, where Cook liberated five geese from the Cape of Good Hope in 1773. *(J. Hall-Jones)*

John Boultbee's sketch of the medal he found on Indian Point in 1825, showing the head of King George IV, the *Resolution* and *Adventure*. *(Boultbee papers)*

Woodhen Cove, just a short distance across a narrow isthmus from Goose Cove. *(J. Hall-Jones)*

The mouth of the Alarm (Seaforth) River at Supper Cove. *(J. Hall-Jones)*

sign of the geese. It is probably significant that a few minutes walk across the narrow isthmus from Goose Cove to the sea is Woodhen Cove, so named by Cook because he found "an immense number of wood-hens" there. As Richard Henry later observed the woodhen are "most outrageous egg-eaters". The tame Cape of Good Hope geese didn't stand a chance.

Continuing his survey to Supper Cove at the head of the sound, Cook and his men camped for the night on the bank of the Seaforth River. At daybreak next morning the duck-shooters among the party blasted off at some waterfowl, at which thunderous sounds a group of very startled Maori leapt up from the tussocks on the opposite side of the river, setting up a "most hideous noise". Cook was eventually able to establish contact with the Maori, but it seems a pity that Cook's original and meaningful name of Alarm River was later changed by Sir Thomas Mackenzie to the Seaforth River.

Departure from Dusky Bay

On their way back to the *Resolution* Cook discovered a "New Passage" out

Passage Point (left) at the entrance to Cook's "New Passage" (Acheron Passage). Resolution Island silhouetted in sunset. *(J. Hall-Jones)*

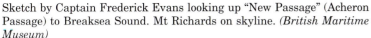

Sketch by Captain Frederick Evans looking up "New Passage" (Acheron Passage) to Breaksea Sound. Mt Richards on skyline. *(British Maritime Museum)*

Muscle Cove, at the entrance to Wet Jacket Arm, where Johann Forster became "very ill" due to eating "muscles". *(J. Hall-Jones)*

to sea (later renamed the Acheron Passage) which "offered a better outlet to the north than the one I came in by". It was now five weeks since the *Resolution* had moored alongside Astronomer Point and Cook had fulfilled all his objectives. He had rested his men, restocked the larder with fresh food and obtained the observations for his chart of "Dusky Bay". Modestly calling his chart "a sketch", it is a brilliant piece of work and in some places more accurate than the subsequent *Acheron* survey.

On 30 April, after loading everything on board including the sheep, setting fire to the dead wood and sowing a variety of garden seeds, including peas and strawberries, the *Resolution* departed Astronomer Point for the "New Passage" out to sea.

After being detained by the lack of wind at Detention Cove on Long Island and Passage Point at the entrance of the "New Passage", they sailed up the channel as far as Wet Jacket Arm, which Pickersgill and the Forsters explored to its head in an open rowing boat. "It began to rain", records George Forster, and "and wetted us to the skin", giving us the origin of the name of Wet Jacket

Arm. When the rain turned to a thunderstorm they landed in a cove at the entrance to the arm. "I became very ill with rheumatic pains", continues Forster, "for I did not like the muscles [mussels] we had", which explains their peculiar name of "Muscle Cove" for this bay. A meaningful name which the author, through the Geographic Board, has had restored to the map.

Continuing up New Passage to Breaksea Sound (a later name by the *Acheron* survey) Cook wondered if Breaksea Sound might be connected to Doubtful Sound. Running out of time to explore it to its head he left it open on his chart as "Nobody Knows What" – a rare display of humour for Cook. After sending Joseph Gilbert, the master, to examine the passage out to sea, the *Resolution* sailed past the Gilbert Islands and Breaksea Island and so on to the Marlborough Sounds.

Cook left a legacy of place-names in "Dusky Bay", many after birds or events while surveying the fjord and fortunately these have been retained. Historic Astronomer Point has been marked with a plaque and the Department of Conservation (DOC) now has a boardwalk round the point to view the fragile remains of the stumps, the outlines of which have been retained by a thick overgrowth of protective kidney fern. A few old cut rata logs can be seen at the boardwalk landing and at the site of New Zealand's first brewery. The New Zealand Navy has marked the site of William Wales' observatory on the crest of the point with a survey station, appropriately with the numbering 1773.

Dr Archibald Menzies, surgeon-botanist to Vancouver's expedition, who gives a lively account of his trips in Dusky Sound in 1791. *(Linnean Society, London)*

"Nobody Knows What"

18 years later, in 1791, midshipman George Vancouver returned to "Dusky Bay", this time as Captain Vancouver in command of *HMS Discovery* and *HMS Chatham* (Lieutenant W. R. Broughton). On 2 November 1791 the two ships anchored just inside the entrance to the fjord, but while the captains were searching for a safer anchorage their ships were caught in a sudden, vicious storm. The two captains just made it to the *Discovery* as she was blown across to Anchor Island Harbour. The little *Chatham* crawled into Facile Harbour and both vessels rode out the storm in their respective havens. In Facile Harbour the "brewing utensils" were put ashore and a "Brewery" (the second brewery in New Zealand) "was established near the Tent".

The "enchanting" inner sanctuary of Sportsmans Cove, Cooper Island. Note tall rimu trees which encompass this secluded cove. *(J. Hall-Jones)*

During the next three weeks they visited many of the coves charted by Cook and completed what little work he had left undone. Fortuitously the expedition's surgeon-botanist, Dr Archibald Menzies, kept a journal which gives us a lively account of their time in Dusky Sound. He records how they searched for the geese in Goose Cove, but could find no sign of them. Finding a Maori "hut" there, they added a little thatch to the framework of sticks and slept the night inside on a bed of ferns. They kindled "a large fire at the entrance to keep off the sand-flys", and were woken in the morning by the "wild heterogeneous chorus" of the birds. Although they came across several other "huts" around the Sound, Menzies noted a "singular absence" of Maori, a contrast to Cook's experience.

The Shag Islands, where Menzies found a "Shagery in the trees". *(J. Hall-Jones)*

Like Sparrman, Menzies enjoyed these little jaunts around the Sound, where on Saturday nights there was always "a hearty bumper of grog". He also played his part in stocking the ship's larder and on one occasion he shot a dozen and a half poy birds (tuis) within 20 metres of the landing. The next day "the birds were dressed in a pie and were allowed by all to be the most delicate and savoury food" yet tasted in this country. He also wounded a parrot (either a kaka or a kea) and the "hideous noise" it made attracted a number of its fellow-feathered friends which fell to his gun.

"Shaping our course for Cooper's Island", continues Menzies, "we found a Shagery in Trees on the Shag Islands, where we killed a few of them". (These would be pied shags which still nest there today.) "Afterwards we went into Sportsmans Cove, an enchanting spot. Here we made a fire, cooked some fish and game and enjoyed a rural repast." (Encompassed by tall rimu trees, this secluded sanctuary is still an "enchanting spot".)

"Captain Vancouver", records Menzies, "now proposed to visit the furthermost branch of the Sound [Nobody Knows What], where Captain Cook left off his survey, in order to [solve] its termination". Passing through "Resolution Passage" (an interesting variation of Cook's name, New Passage) they camped for the night at "Beachy Harbour" (Beach Harbour). Continuing up the fjord they reached Third Cove, the furthest extent of Cook's survey, to discover that his "Apparent Island" was "a narrow point" (Chatham Point) rising steeply from the sea and dividing the fjord into two arms. Vancouver explored the left (northern) arm (Vancouver Arm) to its end, while Menzies with Lieutenant Broughton examined the right (southern) arm (Broughton Arm) to its head. Menzies was impressed by the distinctive granite domes of Broughton Arm and describes "the steep and craggy sides of the lofty mountains" as providing "a wild and romantic scene". Arriving back at their arranged rendezvous on a small island off Chatham Point, the two expeditions agreed that they had proved beyond any doubt that neither arm connected with Doubtful Sound to the north. Continuing down the fjord they camped for the night at Sunday Cove where "we drank a cheerful

Right: The distinctive granite domes of Broughton Arm which so impressed Menzies. *(J. Hall-Jones)*

Left: Chatham Point, encircled by mist, which divides the V-shaped Vancouver Arm of Breaksea Sound (straight ahead) from Broughton Arm (round to the right). *(J. Hall-Jones)*

glass to the memory of Captain Cook, who has left us so little to finish" and reflected "with admiration on the accuracy of his delineations throughout every part of the complicated survey of this extensive Sound".

Before departing from "Dusky Bay" they landed at Astronomer Point where they visited "the eminence on which the Observatory had been pitched". Although the point "was indeed clear of large trees" it was now "covered thickly with brushwood and tall ferns so as to hide the mark of the axe and saw, without diligent searching". Although they "searched attentively for the Garden" they could not find "the least trace of remains of it".

Menzies had gathered a "vast variety of ferns and mosses such as I have never seen before, two tribes of plants that I am particularly fond of". It was a much larger collection than that of the two Forsters, who had twice the amount of time in Dusky Sound, but then Menzies was of the Scottish Highlands and the Forsters were of the city. Amongst Menzies large collection, which he later presented to Kew Gardens, were two fine native trees, the silver beech *Nothofagus menziesii)* and the grass tree *(Dracophyllum menziesii)*.

After changing Cook's name of "Nobody Knows What" to "Somebody Knows What" Vancouver sailed away to carry out his great coastal survey of the west coast of Canada, where his work is immortalised in the names of Vancouver Island and the city of Vancouver.

Cook's suspicion that Dusky Sound might be linked to Doubtful Sound was simply accepted as fact by Lieutenant Thomas McDonnell in his highly inaccurate map of New Zealand. Completely overlooking Vancouver's work and without going there to check for himself, McDonnell linked "Nobody Knows What" to Doubtful Sound with a non-existent "Mac's Passage". In doing so he created a non-existent island, "Patterson Island".

In 1851 the *Acheron* surveyors expunged McDonnell's grossly erroneous "Mac's Passage" and "Patterson Island" from the map and paid tribute to Vancouver's work by naming Vancouver Arm and Broughton Arm. The main

Captain George Vancouver who explored Cook's "Nobody Knows What" in Breaksea Sound in 1791. *(National Portrait Gallery)*

A CLUSTER OF FIRSTS IN NEW ZEALAND

As a direct result of Cook's excellent chart of "Dusky Bay" the early sealers were attracted to its rocky shores and so we find a cluster of firsts in this wild, remote corner of New Zealand. The first two European settlements in New Zealand, albeit one of them an involuntary one, the first European houses, the first ship-building and more ignominiously, the first shipwreck. At one stage there were more Europeans living in Dusky Sound than the whole of the rest of the country, in a region which is now totally uninhabited. Thanks

Luncheon Cove, from the stony beach where the schooner, *Providence,* was built. The narrow entrance to the cove is behind the bow of the *Milford Wanderer.* *(J. Hall-Jones)*

Sound they called Breaksea Sound after Cook's Breaksea Island at the entrance. Their name of Macdonell Island in Doubtful Sound was probably more of a reminder than a memorial to the unscrupulous lieutenant who was notorious for stealing other people's work for 'his' chart of New Zealand.

During the 1890s Richard Henry explored "Mac's Passage" to find that it was a formidable ridge "2,400 feet high", separating the two Sounds. After ascending a steep ridge from the Vancouver Arm side he found that he was looking down sheerly on to Hall Arm. "It is awfully steep and rough country", he wrote, "utterly useless except for climbers".

to the archaeologists Dr Ian Smith, Karl Gillies and their team we now know much more about these unique goings on.

The master-carpenter, Thomas Moore, who built the schooner. *(St Andrews Church, Sydney)*

The first European House and Ship-building

With the intention of obtaining a cargo of sealskins for trade with China, Captain William Raven sailed the *Britannia* into Dusky Sound in November 1792. He soon found that Cook's Luncheon Cove on Anchor Island was the ideal spot to leave his sealing gang. With its narrow entrance and surrounding ridges it was protected from all four winds. There was a good source of freshwater from a stream at the head of the cove and the stony beach at its mouth would be a good place to build a boat. Most importantly, just outside the entrance were the Seal Islands, with a thriving population of seals.

William Leith, the second mate, offered to remain behind in charge of a party of eleven volunteers, one of whom was a key person, the ship's carpenter Thomas Moore. For over a fortnight all hands from the *Britannia* were employed in building a house for the sealing gang.

Thatched with flax leaves, New Zealand's first European house was of substantial proportions "40 feet long, 18 feet wide and 15 feet high". Robert Murry, the fourth officer on the *Britannia*, informs us in his journal that they also constructed "another house, a drying room". Before departing, Captain Raven unloaded 12 months' provisions and enough equipment to build an ocean-going vessel in case the *Britannia* was lost at sea and the gang was left marooned!

Happily the *Britannia* did return 10 months later, in December 1892, and Captain Raven was highly impressed with the schooner which lay on the stocks, almost finished, in the tiny stony inlet at the mouth of the stream. "The carpenter [Thomas Moore] has great merit and has built her with great strength and neatness which few shipwrights belonging to the merchant service are capable of performing", wrote Captain Raven. "53 feet long and of 70 tons burden", the first ship built in New Zealand was later to play a vital role when New Zealand's first shipwreck occurred in Dusky Sound.

Although he was pleased with the vessel Captain Raven was not quite so happy about the sealskins which numbered only 4,500! Re-embarking the sealing gang Captain Raven sailed away leaving the unfinished vessel on the stocks.

Archaeological Investigation in 1997

There has never been any real doubt as to where the 53 foot long schooner was built. The tiny stony inlet at the mouth of the stream at the head of Luncheon Cove is really the only place where a schooner of this size could be constructed. The surviving evidence of this is a rectangular heap of stones at the mouth of the stream which, as pointed out to me by a Shetland ship-builder, is a typical tidal platform to give more elevation to the keel while constructing a ship in a tidal zone. Also, an old rata tree overhanging the inlet has been cut to allow the schooner to fit in more neatly.

An impression by the artist, Gainor Jackson, of the schooner being built in the stony inlet in Luncheon Cove. Also the thatched house, which is now believed to have been sited further up the gully. *(Courtesy G. Jackson, 1985)*

Man-made tidal platform on which the keel of the schooner was laid. *(J. Hall-Jones)*

Once thought to be a drainage ditch from the house, this is now known to be a ventilation shaft for the forge at its head. *(J. Hall-Jones)*

Concerning the site of the house it was the so-called "drainage ditch" about 20 metres upstream on the left bank of the stream that led the Begg brothers to believe that this was the location. Thanks to the archaeological excavations of Ian Smith, Karl Gillies and their team in 1997 we now know otherwise. After excavating the pit at the head of the "drainage ditch" they concluded that this was the site of the forge and firebox, and not the house. Numerous pieces of metal, clinker and charcoal were recovered from there. Also a mast collar, or goose-neck, important evidence linking the site with the ship-building construction. Four glazed fragments of a jar, or mug, found at the site were hand-painted in black writing. When joined together they seemed to include the word "Street", suggesting that it was either the manufacturer's or retailer's address. The glaze and style of writing on these fragments were quite unlike ceramics found in 19th century sites, suggesting that they belonged to the late 18th century.

Concerning the so-called "drainage ditch" from the pit, the excavation revealed that it had a rise in the middle, demonstrating clearly that it was not for drainage, but a trench for providing draft for the firebox and also for raking out the ashes from the fire.

On the opposite side of the stream from the forge the archaeologists excavated another pit which revealed many pieces of charcoal, wood chips and a greasy layer, all of which suggested that this was a "firepit" and that the ship-builders were using seal fat to fuel the fire. Robert Murry in his journal refers to a "a trypot and steam", presumably a whalepot for boiling water for a steambox, which the ship-builders would need for bending the planks to fix around the frame of the ship. For these reasons the archaeologists concluded that a trypot and steambox had once been positioned over the firepit.

As for signs of the house, a large hand-forged iron hinge was found on the hillside north of the firepit. Apart from this hinge no other evidence of a house was found there or anywhere else around luncheon Cove. "It being a thatch-covered building it is very unlikely that it would have been constructed in the immediate vicinity of the fire-risk areas of the forge and firepit", Ian Smith points out, "but in our view a large flat area about 20 metres north of the forge is a highly probable location. However no obvious signs were found there. On the other hand the chances of finding any remains of a thatched construction are now most unlikely. It was an ephemeral house."

The site of the wooden hut on the point above the ship-building inlet was also excavated. A photograph of this hut taken in 1922 by T. Double was given to me some years ago, with a note that it was built of timber taken from the wreck of the *Waikare* on nearby Stop Island in 1910. Although the hut has now rotted away the residual circle of stones and ash there proved to be the fireplace and chimney remains of the hut and were consistent with it being early 20th century.

Fragments of a jar, or mug, recovered by the archaeologists from the vicinity of the forge. Note the apparent word "Street" hand-painted on it. *(Courtesy Dr I. Smith and K. Gillies)*

Hut constructed of wood from the wreck of the *Waikare*. The hut was on the point above the ship-building inlet on left. Photographed in 1922. *(T. Double)*

The first Shipwreck in New Zealand

There was something fishy about Captain William Bampton's departure from Sydney for Dusky Bay in the East Indiaman *Endeavour* in September 1795. Before sailing, Captain Bampton apparently struck a secret deal (no price is known) with Captain Raven for the schooner on the stocks at Luncheon Cove, which he planned to complete and continue on to India with a load of spars for sale to the British Navy. Included in the deal, and unbeknown to him, was the transfer of fourth officer Robert Murry who had a special knowledge of the whereabouts of the unfinished schooner.

It seems incredible that no sooner had the 800 ton *Endeavour* and the 150 ton *Fancy* (also owned by Bampton, but skippered by Captain Thomas Dell) sailed from Sydney that it was 'suddenly' discovered that there were 41 stowaways on board! Although most of them were either escaped convicts or Army deserters there was no suggestion of returning these illegal emigrants to Sydney. There were also 53 extra crewmen and 50 passengers (including two women and three children) on board, bringing the total to 244 persons on the two ships. A goodly number who could be put to work 'if' such a situation arose! It also seems unbelievable that it was only after the arrival of badly leaking *Endeavour* in Facile Harbour that it was 'discovered' that "her stern was entirely decayed and the remaining parts were in so bad a condition that it was a miracle that she held together", as Robert Murry records. Although there is no mention of the *Endeavour* being heavily insured, this late 'discovery' of her shocking state does raise the question.

At this seemingly late stage the *Endeavour* was condemned and they began to unload her. In the process two cannons were tipped off the raft, to remain at the bottom of the harbour until they were salvaged in 1984. On 26 October 1795 a northerly gale blew up tossing the *Endeavour* about and after midnight when she struck a rock she rolled wildly. They hauled her inshore as far as they could and there she settled permanently on the bottom. It was then that all the extra people 'suddenly' became useful. Everyone was employed in stripping the *Endeavour* of anything useful and putting it on shore. Also, in felling trees and cutting timber to convert the lifeboat and to build a dwelling and storehouse.

Captain William Bampton, whose voyage to Dusky Sound in the *Endeavour* was not entirely above board. *(Mitchell Library)*

Meantime Robert Murry had taken Captain Bampton and Captain Dell round to Luncheon Cove to see the schooner on the stocks. "The wharf was still standing", Murry records, "but [it] was knocked off the posts which supported it by the carelessness of [our] boat's crew. We caught a few fish in the entrance of the cove which we fried and ate in the House. The House had, thro' the violence of the weather, lost part of its thatch. [Inside] were a number of casks, one half full of salt. The Trypot and steam [box] were as they were left. The plank which had covered the vessell and drying House, had a part blown off, but was sound. Some of the planks of the vessell had shrunk and a plank or two on the bows had rent." (The *Endeavour* had brought some extra planks from Sydney to complete the ship.)

Returning to the wreck Murry found that "the whole of the Europeans were employed on shore, felling timber for building a store house, on a stony beach opposite to where the ship lay". In describing this scene of activities Murry omits one vital work "end", which has misled everyone to thinking that the stranded party's storehouse and dwelling were literally opposite the wreck. Later we shall see how the archeologists found the remains of these structures at the far end of the stony beach, some 300 metres along the beach to the north.

Murry was now occupied in "cutting flax to thatch the House" (i.e. the dwelling as distinct from the storehouse), but this proved to be in sparse supply, so he then applied his ingenuity to constructing "Murry's Patent Saw Pitt". This was an above ground saw pit in which he laid the logs on six barrels and rigged shears at either end (see sketch). The patent saw pit was so successful that he was soon rigging shears for a second pit.

Within three months the schooner, appropriately named the *Providence,* was completed and ready to sail. Captain Bampton took over command of the *Fancy* and arranged to take 64 people with him. He gave the ousted Captain Dell the *Providence,* ordering him to take 90 people on this much smaller vessel. Then on 7 January 1796 the two ships sailed for Norfolk Island, leaving

An impression by the artist Gainor Jackson of the *Endeavour* aground in Facile Harbour, the *Fancy* astern and the completed schooner *Providence* closer inshore. One of the woman passengers is in the lifeboat to be converted to the *Assistance. (Courtesy G. Jackson, 1985)*

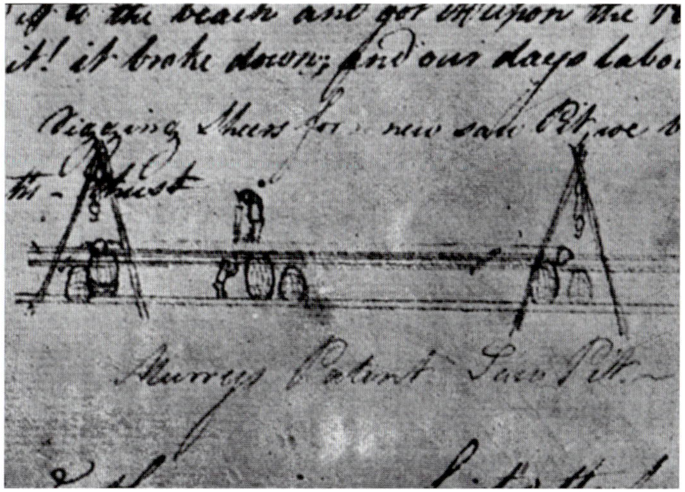

Left: Sketch by Robert Murry of his "Patent Saw Pitt". *(R. McNab)*

Right: Piece of copper-plated teak planking salvaged from the wreck. Also tarred canvas and 8 inch copper spike-nail. *(G. Todd)*

Below: Photograph by Richard Henry, taken in an unusually low tide in 1904, showing the *Endeavour*'s ballast stones out of the water, close inshore. *(AJHR)*

Raising one of the missing cannons of the *Endeavour* in 1984. *(Dr S. Cotton)*

90 people behind in the charge of Mr Waine, the *Endeavour's* first officer, who had had the temerity to argue with his captain. Before they departed Captain Bampton decreed that Waine take the remaining 90 stranded people in the rebuilt longboat, a physical impossibility. Waine eventually sailed in the *Assistance,* as he called the longboat, taking as many as he could, but this still left 35 stranded souls behind. In a fine display of seamanship Waine sailed the little boat all the way to Sydney. The residual 35, after 20 months marooned in Dusky Sound, were rescued in 1797 on the initiative of Governor Hunter (not Captain Bampton) by Captain Todd of the American brig *Mercury.*

Mouth of the stream at the "landing place" of the *Endeavour* settlement. *(J. Hall-Jones)*

The Wreck

As time went by people began to confuse the East Indiaman with Cook's *Endeavour*, so in 1878 Captain John Fairchild of the government steamer service surveyed the wreck:

"She is 128 feet long and about 32 feet beam", he reported.

"Her plank is 5 inches thick, all East India teak. She is sheathed with pure copper and all the bolts used in building her are pure copper also. She is built about one-third of English oak and two-thirds teak. Her stern is in about 20 feet of water and her bow is in 5 feet only. She has freestone [Sydney sandstone] for ballast. She has been known to the whalers [for years] who used to chop her away for firewood and they have now chopped her down to the water's edge."

The wreck was obviously not Cook's barque. It was the eminent historian Robert McNab, who discovered Robert Murry's journal in America, who solved the mystery. Pillaging continued for many years and in 1896 Sir Thomas Mackenzie removed "some pieces of tarred canvas, which although it had lain a hundred years under water, was still fresh and strong".

The position of the wreck in Facile Harbour is demonstrated clearly in a photograph by Richard Henry, taken in an unusually low tide in 1904, showing the ballast stones out of the water. On a calm day this huge mountain of pale Sydney sandstone can still be seen lying on the bottom of the sea, close into shore.

In 1984 the two missing cannons that had tipped of the raft were located by

Collapsed chimney of the house where the *Endeavour*'s onshore party lived. Note that it includes blocks of sandy-coloured ballast stones from the wreck. *(J. Hall-Jones)*

Closer look at one of the blocks of pale Sydney sandstone from the wreck. *(J. Hall-Jones)*

a diving expedition led by Dr Simon Cotton and Kelly Tarlton. They were found lying in 20 metres of water, about 300 metres NE of the wreck. The two 1.5 ton cannons were raised by the expedition and one is now on exhibition at the Fiordland National Park Centre in Te Anau; the other in the Southland Museum.

The Settlement

Until only recently everyone has looked for signs of the *Endeavour* settlement on the shore behind the wreck, but without success. The burnt off bush in Richard Henry's photograph proved a red herring and nothing was found there.

Once again it is thanks to the archaeologists Ian Smith, Karl Gillies and their team that we now know where the settlement was. Using a metal detector they surveyed along the boulder beach to the north of the wreck for about 300 metres, where they came to a stream flowing out onto a fine gravel beach.

At the mouth of the stream, on its south side, were two terraces connected by a line of five steps. The dominant feature of the upper terrace was a pile of large stones which included blocks of Sydney sandstone, linking the structure to the wreck. Noting that the largest of the stones were at the base of the pile and were neatly and tightly stacked, the archaeologists concluded that the pile was a collapsed chimney. At the edge of the chimney was a layer of tightly packed small stones, a cobblestone floor. Artefacts removed from the chimney pile included a knife blade, a piece of unglazed earthenware and a bottle top with a very crudely rolled lip belonging to the late 18th century. With all this evidence the archaeologists concluded that they had found the house where the *Endeavour's* onshore party had lived. (With the benefit of hindsight the stream, an all important source of freshwater, provided a vital clue for earlier searchers.)

On the terrace below the house the archaeologists found a large number of nails, one of which was attached to a piece of wood and they concluded that these were the remains of Robert Murry's "storehouse". It was "framed of wood cut on the spot [from his patent saw pit]", he records, "and sheathed in plank recovered from Luncheon Cove".

Large piece of squared ship's timber at the "landing place", where the *Endeavour*'s longboat was converted. *(J. Hall-Jones)*

Remains of heavily eroded jetty pile at the "landing place". *(J. Hall-Jones)*

Robert Murry's two "patent saw pitts" were probably on the flat alongside the stream at the head of the gravel beach. A large piece of squared ship's timber was found eroding out of the bank there, also a large splitting wedge, indicating that this was the "landing place" where the *Endeavour's* longboat was lengthened and converted into an ocean-going vessel. On the beach at one end of the "saw pitt" flat the archaeologists found a heavily eroded jetty pile, with a notch just below the surface in keeping with an angle brace. Further evidence that this was Murry's "landing place".

About 80 metres back along the boulder beach towards the wreck the archaeologists discovered fragments of barrel hoops lying on the beach and also on the bank above, indicating that this was where the *Endeavour* landed and stockpiled casks from the wreck. It would be an easy walk from there through the bush to the house on the terrace beside the stream.

In conclusion, Dr Smith points out that Luncheon Cove and Facile Harbour have a special place in New Zealand history as the only two places where Europeans constructed onshore settlements before the end of the 18th century. As the archaeological investigation of the first settlement at Luncheon Cove failed to locate the remains of either the first house or drying house, the stone chimney and cobblestone floor at Facile Harbour are the oldest known European constructions still visible in New Zealand.

THE CARETAKER OF RESOLUTION ISLAND

By 1891 the Government had become increasingly concerned about the rapid decline of some bird species, particularly the flightless ones, and Resolution Island was set aside as a bird sanctuary in the hope of giving them a chance to escape their predators, stoats, ferrets and weasels. In 1894 Richard Henry of Te Anau was appointed the "Caretaker of Resolution Island" with a view to capturing kakapo and kiwi about Dusky Sound and transferring them to the 'safety' of Resolution Island. The salary was not great, $300 a year, but Henry was not one to concern himself about money matters. The Otago Acclimatisation

Photograph from Sandy Bay showing Henry's house on the peninsula and his storehouse on the isthmus. Wekas feeding on the beach. The origin of the piles is unknown. (*Fiordland National Park Board*)

Left: Richard Henry standing outside his boatshed on Pigeon Island, 1900. *Putangi* inside. *(Hocken Library)*

Society assisted considerably by providing him with a 16 foot sailing dinghy, *Putangi,* for his work. As for his young assistant, 18 year old Andrew Burt, Henry was expected to pay him out of his own meagre salary.

Arriving in Dusky Sound on the *Hinemoa* on 19 July 1894 Henry and Burt, with four sailors on the oars, set out to find a suitable site for their house. It was a "furiously windy day" in which "the wind almost took charge in the squalls", but late in the afternoon Henry found a location on Pigeon Island which suited all his requirements. The little island was

Henry's house and storehouse (in foreground). Note neatly kept garden, hedges and pathways. (*Fiordland National Park Board*)

Right: All three buildings at Henry's settlement. The three-roomed house, the storehouse in which he first lived (note capstan in front) and the boatshed. (*Hocken Library*)

close to Resolution Island where he was to release the ground birds and there was smooth water in between the two. "It is an almost perfect site", he reported. "There is a little peninsula facing the north. It is only a couple of hundred yards long, with boat harbours on each side of the neck." (Sandy Bay on the west side and Boat Harbour on the east side.)

"Many tons of timber [for the house] and stores" were unloaded from the *Hinemoa* and the ship's carpenters went ashore to erect a temporary shelter for Henry and Burt, a tent with a boarded floor. But the two soon found that there were scores of rats living on Pigeon Island and the tent was not providing protection from them. "So I built a hut 12 x 10 [feet] up on piles which makes us independent." Later, when they moved into the house, the hut became the storehouse, as seen in photographs.

Putangi needed the protection of a boatshed, so after creating a clearing in the bush just above the high water mark in Boatshed Bay (as they now called it) they erected a rough boatshed thatched on the sides. A slipway and carriage with trolley wheels were constructed and later Henry installed a capstan to help haul *Putangi* out of the sea. Depending on the

Remains of the brick chimney of Henry's house. (*J. Hall-Jones*)

Richard Henry's "punga paddock" for kiwis. (*J. Hall-Jones*)

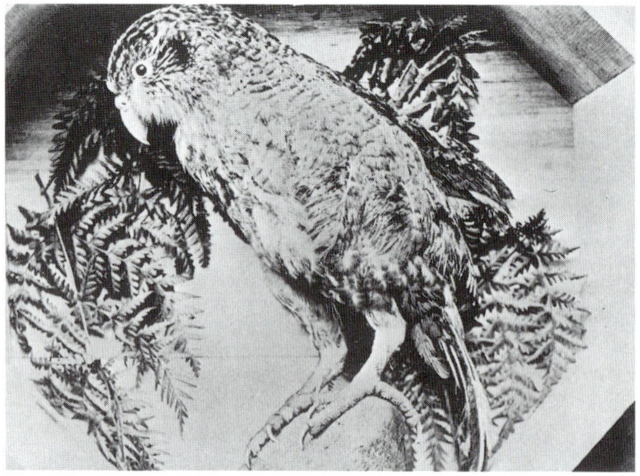

Left: Photograph of kakapo by Richard Henry. (*AJHR*)

direction of the wind *Putangi* could also be landed at Sandy Bay on the opposite side of the isthmus. (Concerning the rows of piles there, their origin remains unknown, but some squared holes on their tops would suggest that at some time someone had planked them for a wharf.) They also dug a vegetable garden and a photograph shows how they created pathways, neatly lined with hedges.

Choosing a site for the house in the lee of the hill on the peninsula, Henry began to build his home. Constructed of weatherboards, with a corrugated iron roof and a solid brick chimney, it had a kitchen-sitting room 20 x 10 feet and two bedrooms 10 x 10 feet. By the end of 1894 it was finished and painted outside. Later a cupboard, two tables and two chairs were added to the sitting room and the walls papered. A water tank and spouting were installed because of the lack of freshwater on Pigeon Island.

A few metres beyond the house he later created a "little paddock for roas [large kiwis] out of pungies, because they worry so much [tangling their long bills] trying to get through the netting [of the cages]. Also a dark house for them to avoid sandflies." This was in contrast to the kakapo who accepted the netted cages quite placidly, as long as there were not two males in one, in which case they fought!

In 1965, when I first visited the site of Richard Henry's little settlement, there were still some remains of his boatshed at the back of Boatshed Beach, also the wooden rails of his tramline and a pair of wheels for his trolley carriage. The house's corrugated iron roof had been removed for scrap metal during the War and the house burnt down. But some wooden piles were still in place, also the massive base of the brick chimney. Various pieces of bottles, jars and crockery lay about and, interestingly, some glass photograph plates, visible evidence that he photographed the flightless birds that he was capturing and that he developed the plates himself in his own dark room. The rectangular "punga paddock" for kiwis was heavily overgrown. Fortunately this unique structure has survived and is now looked after carefully by DOC, which has also reopened Henry's track across to his lookout on the south side of the island, where he escaped from the sandflies and could keep an eye out for ships entering Dusky Sound.

Concerning Richard Henry's 15 years work in Dusky Sound trying to save the flightless birds from extinction, this has been recorded by Susanne and John Hill in their excellent book *Richard Henry of Resolution Island* which is strongly recommended to anyone wishing to learn more about this remarkable and resourceful man.

Henry had a flair for recording his penetrating observations with his distinctive, pithy phrases. His term of "pit dwellers" for the Maori of Indian Island and his description of "Mac's Passage" as being "utterly useless except for climbers" have been mentioned already. In the same vein he refers to the region as being "fine country for the waterproof explorer". Some of his observations on kakapo are also relevant to this book, particularly as the species is now probably extinct on the Fiordland mainland. Using a muzzled dog he spent many demanding days capturing the kakapo and transferring them to Resolution Island and later other islands, "so that all the eggs may not be in one basket. These old New Zealanders are simple poor things, they cannot fly and they know nothing of enemies of any sort." Watching the kakapo chewing grass, he describes them as having the most efficient "milling apparatus" that he had ever seen in birds. After rolling the grass around in this "steel mill" and extracting the nutrients, "they leave the [useless] fibre attached to the remainder of the leaf". (Kakapo chews as they are now called.)

"They form very distinctive pathways, especially going up a small hill. Here on the dry tops will be several 'dusting holes' all connected by well beaten pathways." (A track and bowl system or kakapo arena as we now call it.) Away ahead of his time Henry recognised these 'dusting holes' as display bowls where the male kakapo "distend their air-sacs and start their booming which can be heard for a couple of miles. The females like others of their sex, love the music and come up to see the show." The males start this booming about the end of November, he noted, usually every second year, but not always. "During the off-season these [arenas] are deserted", he observed.

In 1900, after transferring 300-400 kakapo to Resolution Island and other islands, he discovered a "weasel" (stoat) on Resolution Island. Understandably he suffered a fit of the blues and considered tossing the whole project in. But a small rise ($30 per annum!) in his salary set him in high spirits again. "It was not so much the money, but the thought that lay behind it", he comments.

In 1909 after 15 years work transferring a total of 750 flightless birds, mainly kakapo, Henry departed from Dusky Sound, only to take on another lonely job as custodian of Kapiti Island. In 1929 this observant gentle man of nature passed away. His booklet *The Flightless Birds of New Zealand (1903)* is a classic of its kind and records his observations on flightless and other birds during his 25 years at Dusky Sound and Lake Te Anau.

The Old General

Within a month of his arrival on Pigeon Island Richard Henry received a visit from the other hermit of Dusky Sound, the prospector William Docherty.

Boatshed Bay, 1910, showing *Putangi* inside the boatshed, another boat (covered) on the boatshed slip and Henry's launch, *Premier,* on the rails. (*Photograph by Russell Duncan. Courtesy Mrs Janet Menzies*)

Sketch by Herbert Cox showing the location of Docherty's copper lode on Mt Solitary. Also Docherty's original hut, directly below the lode in Shark Cove. (*H. Cox*)

"I heard the rattle of his oars as he rounded the point coming into our little bay", recounts Henry. His caller "evidently did not get himself up into orthodox visiting style for he was very like a wild man. He had two pairs of trousers on, of which only parts of each could be seen in various places, lace up boots without laces, glengary cap, and his shirts were like his pants."

Stepping ashore the old timer (he was 64) stretched out his hand and bade Henry "welcome to Dusky Sound". Henry asked his tattered visitor about the booming of the kakapo in Dusky Sound and was somewhat puzzled to receive the reply that "yes, he had heard the booming sound but believed it was a rumbling in the earth and that he had heard it ever since the explosions of Karakatoa [volcano]. He puzzled me at first", comments Henry, "I do not think he is a fool, but a queer old general". It soon became obvious that the old prospector was on the cadge and by the time he departed he had wheedled stores, tobacco and even half a bottle of whisky out of the generous Henry. On a later visit Docherty endeared himself even less when he called out to Henry, "Fetch your dog, there is a [wood]hen on the beach". Obviously the old general was living on woodhens and indeed he admitted so. This was the last straw as far as Henry, the ranger, was concerned and after this he did his best to discourage visits from his only fellow creature in the Sound. The last thing Henry wanted was to return some day to find that the "queer old general" had been sleeping in his bed!

The rough, tough old prospector arrived in Dusky Sound in 1877 and soon afterwards he discovered a copper lode on the steep cliffs of Mt Solitary, in Shark Cove at the head of the Sound. Geologist Herbert Cox inspected the lode finding that it included "copper pyrites scattered throughout, in places containing up to 23% metallic copper". He advised Docherty to dynamite the lode from below, but the independent old general dynamited too high blowing the lode away, literally. Cox's report includes a sketch of Docherty's original hut in Shark Cove, in the little bay at the southern entrance.

Docherty's house at Docherty's Beach. Note steep shingle roof and huge corrugated iron chimney. (*A. Reischek*)

Right: Docherty's Beach, with Docherty Stream flowing out onto the "beautiful sand and peebled beach". *(J. Hall-Jones)*

Below right: Beach at the head of Wet Jacket Arm where Docherty lived for three months trying to find a route through to Lake Manapouri. *(J. Hall-Jones)*

After this failure Docherty moved over to the north side of the Sound to Docherty's Beach (opposite Cooper's Island) where he built his permanent residence. It was a sturdy timber building with a steep shingle roof and a massive corrugated iron chimney.

Geologist Robert Paulin landed at Docherty's Beach in 1889 and describes "three well-built huts at the back of a beautiful sand and pebble-beached bay through which a limpid stream [Docherty's Creek] empties into the Sound. We found the huts empty except for swarms of sandflies." Paulin followed a "well-made track leading up a gully behind the huts for over two miles". Later that year Bella Hislop, a passenger on the *Stella,* visited "Docherty's house". This time the owner was in residence. "Docherty is a quiet, unsympathetic looking man", records Hislop (maybe he was allergic to tourists) "who makes quite a Man Friday of young Harris [his assistant, a son of John Hyde Harris, Otago's Superintendent], a fine looking fellow of 17. The house is a fair size with three or four bed places round it [inside]. The rafters serve to hang clothes on. There is a grand big fireplace, the best thing in the establishment, with four logs on the fire." (Today the remains of the "grand big fireplace" can still be seen on the bank of the "limpid stream" flowing out onto the "beautiful sand and pebble-beached bay".)

With the failure of his copper lode on Mt Solitary Docherty continued his search for minerals and, with financial assistance from the Government, he cut the "well-made track" up the gully behind his hut onto the open tops of Mt Pender. Thanks to the searchings of geologist Sean O'Hagan we now know more about the prospecting of the old miner on these open tops of Mt Pender. In 1976 Sean rediscovered Docherty's mining pits at the head of Docherty's Creek, on the summit slopes of Mt Pender. Also some tools, a crowbar, a pick-head and a sledge hammer. He collected samples from the pits where Docherty had been working and these proved to contain zinc, not copper as previously thought.

Docherty also attacked Mt Pender from its northern side. Sailing round into Wet Jacket Arm he constructed a rock landing-stage and corrugated iron shelter at the foot of a long slip opposite Oke Island. Then, scrambling up the steep slip on the side of Mt Pender, he began mining at about 500 metres above sea-level. (In 1965 the remains of all these activities were still obvious, including his mine and tools, high on the slip. But the slip has since become heavily

Docherty's grave on Docherty Island, with the totara post carved by ranger Phil Dorizac. (*J. Hall-Jones*)

overgrown and only the rock-wall landing is now left for easy viewing.)

Bella Hislop also records that Docherty had "another residence" in Wet Jacket Arm, at its head. "We landed at another residence of Docherty's", she writes in 1889, "which is in the side of a rock, perfectly sheltered from the wind and rain. He lived here for three months while trying to find a way through to Lake Manapouri." (The large shelter rock is still obvious on the beach at the head of Wet Jacket Arm.)

In spite of all this hard work over the years the old prospector never really made anything from his mineral minings. By 1894 the Preservation Inlet gold rush was at its height and Docherty, after 17 years in Dusky Sound, succumbed to the allure of gold fever. He decided to depart from Dusky and set out in his open dinghy (round which he had rigged barrels as floats), with a bucket of cod heads for food. He is described as arriving at Cromarty "all tied up with wire and string; a well-built man with a grey clipped beard". After prospecting around the inlet for a couple of years, he suddenly (on 20 March 1896) collapsed and died at Cromarty. "He had been laughing and joking with some of his friends a few minutes before", recounts George Biggar. "Kindly hands among the diggers decided to bury him on a pretty little island at Cromarty. The funeral [procession] was an unique one – eight or ten boats laden with diggers. One of the diggers read the burial service, while the hardy diggers in their time-worn garments crowded around." It was a peaceful resting place for the "old general". The way he would have wished it. His grave on Docherty Island (as the island is now known) is marked with a totara post carved by ranger Phil Dorizac. The name Docherty Creek, on the Haast highway, recalls his earlier prospecting on the West Coast.

WILDLIFE

Sealing

Contrary to the law, seals were still being slaughtered in Dusky Sound in the early 1900s,

Right: Remains of sealer's clinker built boat found in Luncheon Cove. (*J. Hall-Jones*)

Below: Seal pup in the seal 'nursery' in Luncheon Cove. (*J. Hall-Jones*)

Remains of whaleboat found at the head of Cascade Cove in 1965. (*J. Hall-Jones*)

in spite of the presence of a ranger. Returning from an expedition, Henry was disgusted to come across a shot seal carcass floating in the sea off Long Island. He later learned that two boats working on the coast took over 200 sealskins in one season.

Regardless of this continued molestation, the seal survives today in Dusky Sound in large numbers. Even in Luncheon Cove, where it all began, there is a thriving seal nursery. Also, outside on the well-named Seal Islands there is a large colony of seals.

In 1965 we discovered part of a sealer's clinker built whaleboat in Luncheon Cove, where Henry had earlier reported the remains of sealers' punga huts. We also found a large wooden boat, rotting on the mudflats at the head of Cascade Cove, with the engine and rudder still in place. Fishermen told us that it had belonged to Captain Harry Roderique of Bluff, who was known to have sealed on this coast in the early 1900s. The boat has since rotted away.

Notornis

The first notornis (takahe) ever seen alive by Europeans was captured in a gully at the back of Duck Cove on Resolution Island in 1849. As Commissioner Walter Mantell reports:

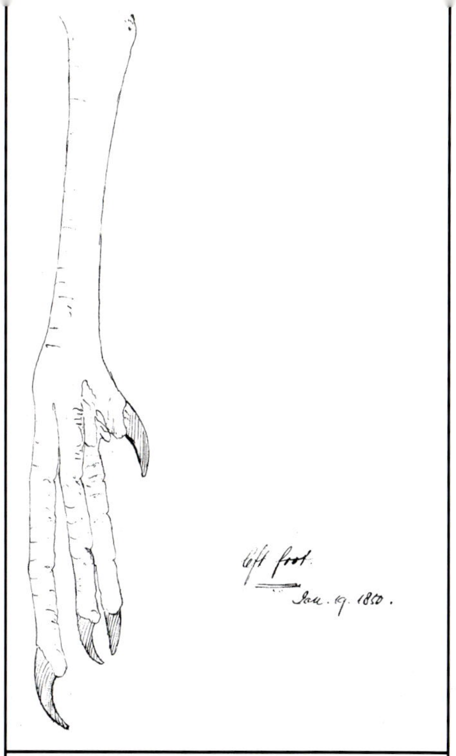

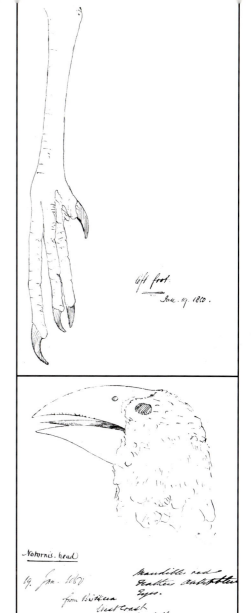

Drawing by Walter Mantell of the head of the first specimen of *Notornis mantelli*, which was caught in Dusky Sound in 1849. (*Mantell papers*)

Top: Drawing by Mantell of the left foot of the first specimen of notornis. (*Mantell papers*)

Stalactites of the limestone overhang on Long Island, where two pieces of leg bone of the large *Euryapteryx* species of moa were found in 1965. (*J. Hall-Jones*)

"This bird was taken by some sealers who were pursuing their avocations in Dusky Bay. Perceiving the trail of a large and unknown bird on the snow with which the ground was then covered [it was winter], they followed the footprints till they obtained a sight of the notornis, which their dogs instantly pursued, and after a long chase caught alive in a gully of a [cove] behind Resolution Island. It ran with great speed, and upon being captured uttered loud screams, and fought and struggled violently; it was kept alive three of four days on board the schooner and then killed, and the body roasted and eaten by the crew, each partaking of the dainty, which was declared to be delicious. The beak and legs were of bright red colour."

Fortunately the sealers retained the remains of the "large and unknown bird" after their feast and presented these to Walter Mantell, who had previously discovered the skull of a notornis in a moa-hunter's midden in the North Island and had assumed that the species was extinct. After making drawings of the head and left leg, Mantell packed these carefully with the skin and sent them to his father, Dr Gideon Mantell in London. Dr Mantell offered this first ever specimen of *Notornis mantelli* to the British Museum, who rejected it initially and only accepted it after Dr Mantell had had it stuffed and mounted at his own expense. This first specimen of notornis is now in the British Museum of Natural History in London.

Moa

One of the most exciting finds of our Canterbury Museum expedition to Dusky Sound in 1965 was to discover two pieces of leg bone from the large *Euryapteryx* species of moa, a species which had not previously been reported in Fiordland. We discovered the two bones in a large Maori midden beneath a limestone overhang at the west end of Long Island, opposite the "pits" of Indian Point. Suspecting that they were moa bones we sent them to Ron Scarlett, New Zealand's authority on moa bones, who confirmed that they were two pieces of the left tibio-tarsus (leg bone) of *Euryapteryx gravis.* Because of the total absence of any other bones of this species in the oven, or anywhere else in Fiordland, Ron Scarlett postulated that the leg bone had been brought round from the eastern grasslands for eating, in the same way that today we would take a cooked leg of mutton.

South Island Kokako

Thanks to George Forster we have a painting of a South Island kokako (orange-wattled crow) which he shot in Cascade Cove. "A large wattle-bird was killed by my son", writes Johann Forster. "It is the size of a pigeon and dark blueish grey [in colour]. It has a large orange yellow wattle which is blue at its insertion at the corner of the mouth. Compared with the shrill note of the smaller birds, the wattle bird has a graver pipe", he noted.

Painting of South Island kokako (orange-wattled crow) by George Forster in 1773. (*British Museum Natural History*)

On his visit to Dusky Sound in 1889 Robert Paulin found that the "native crows" were still numerous. "They are more like magpies than crows in shape, are black in colour and [have] yellow wattles. They do not fly, but hop to a great distance."

The orange-wattled crows were still about when Richard Henry arrived in 1894, but by the time he departed in 1909 he noticed that they were on the decline. With reluctance he acceded to the demand of the Governor-General Lord Ranfurly to provide two specimens for his private collection.

In 1965 Alan Picard and I were woken at dawn by a beautiful, melodious 'bong' sound just outside our tent in Cascade Cove. Both of us agreed that it was a sound that neither of us had ever heard before. It was only after Rhys Buckingham rediscovered the South Island kokako (which was thought to have become extinct) and I heard his taped kokako calls that I realised that these calls were identical to what we had heard in Cascade Cove. For the want of a little more energy and rousing ourselves, we could have seen a kokako outside our tent.

South Island Thrush (Piopio)

Thanks to Johann Forster we have a good description of a South Island thrush which his son, George, shot in Cascade Cove.

"It has a short strong bill, is brown with whitish strokes [stripes] on the belly and breast and has a long ferruginous tail."

Richard Henry gives us a delightful account of a South Island thrush which adopted him in its loneliness:

"There was a native thrush about my house before I went away [in 1898], quite tame; but since my return it has become almost too tame for it comes into the house every chance it gets. It is generally whistling outside before I get up, and when I am at breakfast I lift the window and answer its call; it comes hopping in and about the table, tastes the tea and the milk several times and licks its lips with a critical air. It flies on to the mantelpiece and studies the clock closely. Then on to the carpenter's bench, where it looks into everything, even down the spout of an old teapot.

It is good company on account of its singular tameness, or ignorance of these progressive times [of predation]. It is evidently lost or in search of a mate, and that is why it comes so readily when I answer its call. I showed it the looking-glass and it was greatly interested in it. When I stood the glass against the wall on the floor the thrush was delighted with the company at first, but soon seemed to realise that the one in the glass was only mocking it. It called distinctly [at] the shadow and listened for the answer. Then went outside and began to sing to see if that would have any effect.

It is not unlike our old [European] thrush, but more russet in colour, especially the tail, and the spots on the breast are very distinct."

Henry noted that even in his day the native thrush was "not at all plentiful" and that he had "never found a nest". From his description of its "singular tameness" the bird was particularly vulnerable to predators and was soon to become extinct.

Painting of South Island thrush by Anders Sparrman in 1773. (*British Museum*)

Moose from Canada

In 1910 ten moose calves, six males and four females, from Canada were released on the Seaforth River delta at Supper Cove. Hand-reared and thoroughly tame after their long voyage from Vancouver, the young moose were not at all pleased with their new location and promptly returned to their crates! Or perhaps they were driven back by the notorious sandflies of Supper Cove! Eventually the crates were upended and the reluctant calves driven up onto the bank of the river, where the Dusky

Photograph by Les Murrell of two moose in the upper Seaforth River in 1927. (*Weekly Press*)

Track 'roadway' provided open access for several kilometres up the valley. A wide, flat valley with swamps along the 'roadway', it was really the only suitable place in Fiordland to liberate such a large, swamp-grazing and heavily timbered beast.

Within a few days of their release one of the calves was shot at Supper Cove by a fisherman, unaware that they were protected by law. The first moose bull to be shot legally under licence fell to the gun of Eddie Herrick in the lower Seaforth Valley in 1929. Six years later the Hawkes Bay farmer returned to shoot a second bull, this time in Herrick Creek, above Wet Jacket Arm. During 1951 two moose cows were shot, one in Herrick Creek by Jim Mackintosh and the other in the Henry Burn, Supper Cove, by Robin Francis Smith. In 1955 Max Kershaw shot another moose in the Henry Burn, which links the Seaforth Valley with Herrick Creek via a low saddle.

This was thought to be the last of the moose and that the introduced species had become extinct. Then in 1971 Gordon ("Spunky") Anderson supposedly (there was no visible evidence) shot a moose in Herrick Creek. The report aroused the interest of wildlife scientist Ken Tustin who, after many cold wet days in the field, pieced together his evidence that the moose still exists in Dusky Sound. During the 1990s he discovered the characteristic

Jim Mackintosh with cow moose shot in Herrick Creek in 1951. (*J. Mackintosh collection*)

Left: Eddie Herrick with the first bull shot under licence, upper Seaforth Valley, 1929. (*Courtesy, Herrick Family*)

browsing sign and dewclaw footprints of moose in Herrick Creek. The ultimate proof would of course be a photograph. In 1996 his video surveillance camera photographed a large, dark-coloured beast with a rolling gait, that convinced Tustin that he had photographed a moose in Herrick Creek. But maddeningly for Tustin, the tree on which the triggering sensor had been mounted had bent downwards under the weight of snow. As a result there was no clear picture of the head, the final proof that the deer was a moose.

Sunrise over Breaksea Island sanctuary, a modern day Noah's Ark. (*J. Hall-Jones*)

Breaksea Island Sanctuary

A project that would have been dear to Richard Henry's heart was the highly successful rat eradication programme that was carried out on Breaksea Island during 1988-1991. Although Breaksea Island was infested with Norway rats introduced by the sealers, it was chosen as a potential wildlife sanctuary because it was beyond the swimming range of rats and stoats. If only the indigenous rats could be exterminated it would be ideal. With the help of Operation Raleigh volunteers tracks were cut at five different levels round the steep cliffs of Breaksea Island. Tubes, which only rats could enter, were baited with rat poison and laid along these tracks, which were checked daily. After a few days the rat population of several thousand dropped dramatically and eventually the island was declared rat-free.

Interestingly the Fiordland skink, which the rats had all but eliminated, reappeared in large numbers. Two species of weevil were re-introduced and in 1992, 59 saddlebacks from Stewart Island's offshore islands were landed by helicopter and released. In 1995, 30 yellowheads from the Blue Mountains were transferred to the new sanctuary.

Breaksea Island has become a highly prized refuge for endangered species, a modern-day Noah's Ark.

CHAPTER 3

Doubtfull Harbour Explored by Spaniards

We pass'd a small narrow opening with an Island lying in the middle.
James Cook, 14 March 1770

Bauza Island lying plumb in the middle of the entrance of Doubtful Sound. The narrow "Sur" (South) channel on the left and "Norte" (North) Channel on the right. (*J. Hall-Jones*)

After bypassing "Dusky Bay" in the *Endeavour* in 1770, Cook came to a "small narrow opening in the land where there appeared to be a very snug harbour". But there was a large "Island [Bauza Island] lying in the middle of the opening" with only a narrow channel on each side. "The land on each side of the entrance riseth almost perpendicular from the sea to a very considerable height and this was the reason why I did not attempt to go in with the ship, because I saw clearly that no wind could blow there [except] right in [a westerly] or right out [an easterly]." As Cook had noted that easterlies only blew "one day in a month" on the coast he "doubted" the wisdom of sailing the *Endeavour* into this harbour where she could be stuck for a month waiting for an easterly.

In the hinterland behind "Doubtfull Harbour", as Cook called the "snug harbour", rose a great wall of snow-capped mountains. Richard Pickersgill likened the land to the fjords of Norway:

"Hauld up Close to ye Land. Passed by a bay or harbour called Doubtfull Harbour, the Land making high and Ragged like the coast of Noraway, being craggy and Steep."

And so Cook sailed away from "Doubtfull Harbour" in 1770 leaving it named, but unexplored. It was the Spanish expedition under

Captain Alessandro Malaspina, the Italian commander of the Spanish expedition which voyaged round the world (1789-1793), charting Doubtful Sound on the way. (*Museo Naval*)

The Spanish corvettes *Descubertia* and *Atrevida* at Tonga. Note observatory tent erected on point. (*Museo Naval*)

Captain Alessandro Malaspina, who in 1793 became the first Europeans to explore and chart "Doubtfull Harbour".

The Spanish Map

"There was a new softness in the air", longer days and cooler nights, as Captain Alessandro Malaspina headed south from the tropics towards New Zealand with his two Spanish corvettes *Descubierta* (the Discovery) and *Atrevida* (the Bold). On 25 February 1793 he arrived off Febrero Point at the entrance to "Doubtfull Harbour". Heeding Cook's doubts about sailing into Doubtfull Harbour, Malaspina sent the *Descubierta*'s armed boat "to reconnoitre the interior of the harbour", while the two corvettes lay off the entrance. The "armed boat" was placed under the command of the hydrographer, second lieutenant Felipe Bauza, whose orders were to explore the harbour, but to return to the *Descubierta* as soon as possible! Considering that it was not until after midday that Bauza's expedition set out and that he was taking soundings

Febrero Point, where the two Spanish corvettes arrived off the entrance to Doubtful Sound on 25 February 1793. (*J. Hall-Jones*)

all the way, his resultant map is a remarkable piece of work. Small wonder that he later became the Hydrographer of the Spanish Navy.

Bauza dots in the route of the

Marcaciones Point, Bauza Island, site of the first Spanish landing in New Zealand. (*J. Hall-Jones*)

Felipe Bauza, later the Hydrographer of the Spanish Navy, who explored and charted Doubtful Sound in 1793. (*Museo Naval*)

"armed boat" on his chart showing how he departed from the *Descubierta* lying off the outer side of the Hares Ears, and how he took his first and shallowest sounding (15 fathoms) off "25 Febrero Point", the date that they were there. As he approached Bauza Island he spotted a "Cascada" (waterfall) dropping from the "Atlas Montanas" (high mountains) into a little bay (now called Cascada Bay) on the south side of the fjord. Entering the "Sur" Channel on the south side of Bauza Island, they nosed into two points looking for a place to land, but it was not until they reached the very eastern tip of the island that they actually put ashore. Here at Marcaciones Point was a fine sloping rock, easy to land on, and Spaniards stepped ashore for the first time in New Zealand.

Until recently the meaning of the name Marcaciones remained a mystery, but a little research revealed that it was an old nautical term for "measuring

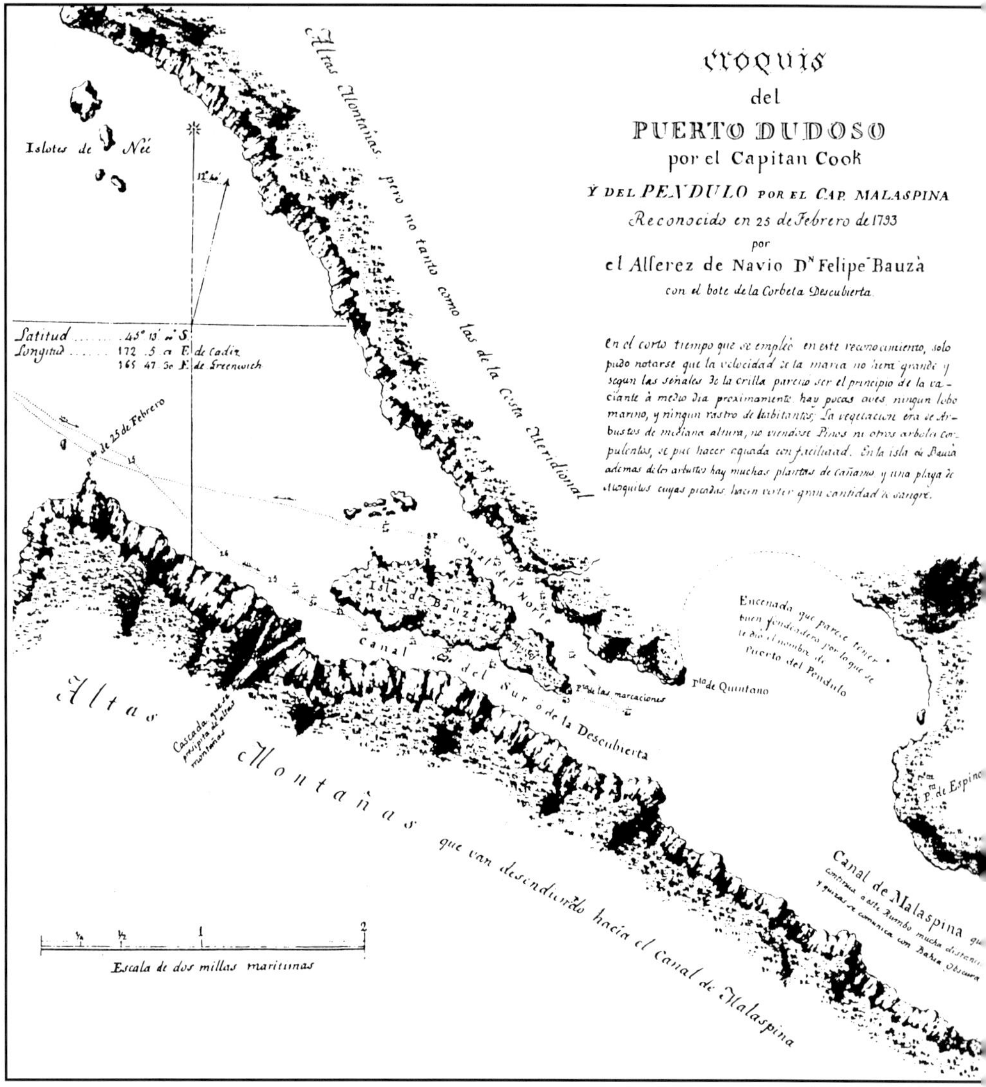

Bauza's chart of Doubtful Sound showing the original Spanish names and the route of his armed boat dotted in. (*J. Hall-Jones*)

angles". Situated at the very eastern tip of Bauza Island, Marcaciones Point gives an excellent unobstructed view straight up the main sound. From the interpretation of the name, Bauza was obviously using the point for taking his observations for his chart and as such, the English equivalent for the name would be Observation Point. As the site of the first Spanish landing in New Zealand and as the observation point for the only Spanish chart of New Zealand, Marcaciones Point is an important landmark in our history. Unaware of the special significance of the name Marcaciones Point, Captain Stokes of the subsequent *Acheron* survey of Doubtful Sound in 1851 changed Bauza's name to the nondescript one of Flurry Head. In 1987 the author through the New Zealand Geographic Board was able to have Bauza's highly important name restored on the map.

While Bauza was taking his observations on Marcaciones Point he and the crew suffered from "a plague of mosquitoes whose bites made us bleed freely". Being daylight, the "mosquitoes" would be sandflies, for which Doubtful Sound is notorious. Whichever, the alternative Spanish name for Bauza Island (as it was deservedly named) was the "Island of Mosquitoes".

Completing his observations, Bauza continued up the fjord for half a kilometre, but by then it was time to turn. If only he had been able to carry on for another half kilometre the whole key of the inner waterways would have been revealed to him. He was able to see the main channel "continuing its course for a great distance and perhaps communicating with Dusky Bay"

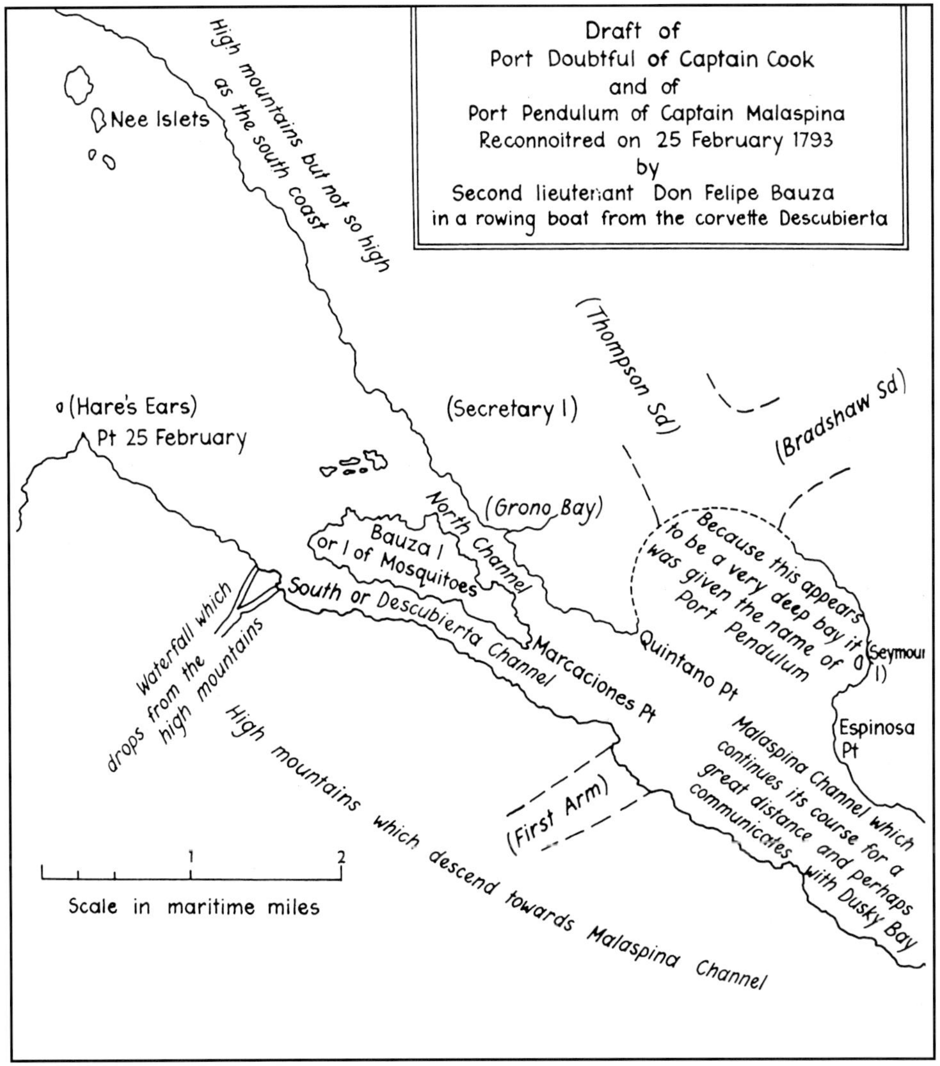

Diagram to show Bauza's annotations on his chart translated into English. The branches that he was unable to see are dotted in and later names are given in brackets. (*Copyright, J. Hall-Jones*)

Captain Malaspina (on right inside tent) with the simple pendulum that he was using to measure differences in gravity around the world. Note scribe standing primly outside. (*Museo Naval*)

(Mac's Passage) and he named this Malaspina Channel after the commander. But he was unable to see the entrance to First Arm leading off to the south. On the north side of the fjord, a prominent point which he named Quintano Point (after third lieutenant Fernando Quintano of the *Descubierta*), concealed Thompson Sound, the northern outlet of Doubtful Sound. Quintano Point also hid the entrance to Bradshaw Sound, an offshoot of Thompson Sound. Unable to see either of these openings he properly closed them off on his chart as a deep bay, but with a dotted line only. He was, however, able to obtain a view of Seymour Island, which he marks, un-named, on his chart as lying off Espinosa Point (which he named after his assistant, Jose Espinosa). The large open 'bay' between Quintano and Espinosa Points he called Port Pendulum, "after the simple pendulum" that Malaspina was using to measure differences in gravity around the world.

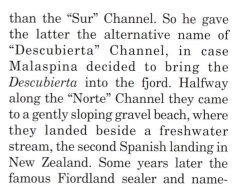

It was now time to head back to the *Descubierta* and continuing round Bauza Island Bauza entered the "Norte" Channel, which he found was shallower than the "Sur" Channel. So he gave the latter the alternative name of "Descubierta" Channel, in case Malaspina decided to bring the *Descubierta* into the fjord. Halfway along the "Norte" Channel they came to a gently sloping gravel beach, where they landed beside a freshwater stream, the second Spanish landing in New Zealand. Some years later the famous Fiordland sealer and name-

Fur seal colony on the Nee Islets, which Bauza named after Luis Nee the botanist aboard the *Atrevida*. (*J. Hall-Jones*)

Left: The Hares Ears at the entrance of Doubtful Sound where Malaspina's corvettes waited while Bauza explored inside. Febrero Point behind, on right. (*J. Hall-Jones*)

giver, Captain John Grono, was to make good use of this same beach as a sealing station and the bay became known as Grono Bay.

At 6 pm they heard a cannon shot from one of the corvettes and they answered by firing the gun of their armed boat. Obviously Malaspina was becoming worried about the expedition and Bauza decided to cut through the Shelter Islands and head straight for the *Descubierta*. On this final leg of his journey Bauza could see the "Nee Islets" lying to their north, where he observed in the distance "sea lions and plenty of birds". (These would be New Zealand fur seals, which are still there in large numbers.) The islets he named after Luis Nee the botanist aboard the *Atrevida*.

It was 9 pm and the sun was setting by the time Bauza arrived back on the *Descubierta* and reported his findings to Malaspina. "There are few birds, no seals [excluding the colony on the Nee Islets] and no sign of any inhabitants", he reported. Later he was to commence work on his remarkable, artistic chart of "Puerto Dudoso, the Port Doubtful of Captain Cook".

On his return to Spain, Bauza continued his career as a cartographer and eventually became the Hydrographer of the Spanish Navy. But his chart of Doubtful Sound remained unpublished. He became a liberal Member of Parliament and then in a political upheaval, he was exiled by the King and sought asylum in England. Fortuitously, Bauza had a number of friends in the British Hydrographic office who greatly admired his special talent in drawing maps and a position was found for him in this office. And so it was that his chart of "Puerto Dudoso" was eventually published by the British Admiralty, not the Spanish Navy, in 1840. But by then Bauza had been dead for six years.

The famous sealer Captain John Grono who explored the inner reaches of Doubtful Sound naming Thompson Sound and Hall Arm. (*K. Brown*)

Freshwater stream in Grono Bay where Grono had a sealing station in "Gronow's". Bauza Island across Norte Channel. (*J. Hall-Jones*)

Gronow's

The first European to follow Bauza into Doubtful Sound was probably the famous sealer Captain John Grono who in 1809 sailed the *Governor Bligh* across from Australia and entered the Sound to establish a sealing station in Grono Bay. With its easy gravel beach to land on, a permanent stream of freshwater and ready access to the seal colonies on the Nee Islets and Shelter Islands, it was an ideal spot for such a base. Exploring more deeply into the Sound than Bauza, he discovered that Port Pendulum was really another outlet to the sea, which he named Thompson Sound after Andrew Thompson, the owner of his ship and his neighbour on the Hawkesbury River in New South Wales. Grono penetrated the Malaspina Channel to its head to discover Elizabeth Island, which he named after his wife, and Hall Arm which he named after his son-in-law George Hall.

It was therefore with some justification that Doubtfull Harbour became

Malaspina Reach which Grono explored, naming Elizabeth Island (on right) after his wife. (*J. Hall-Jones*)

known amongst the sealing fraternity as "Gronow's". The name appears as such on Edward Merurant's sealing map of Fiordland, which also shows "Thompson's" as the northern outlet of the Sound.

The Spanish Names

Bauza left a cluster of twelve Spanish place-names on his chart of Doubtful Sound, which are quite unique, being the only Spanish names on the whole map of New Zealand. In view of this it would seem a pity that Captain Stokes in his survey of Doubtful Sound in 1851 chose to remove nine of them, retaining only Febrero Point, Bauza Island and Nee Islets, misspelling the latter "Nea Islet" and implying that it was a single islet.

Heavy-handedly he renamed the Malaspina Channel, Smith Sound, after J. W. Smith the second master of the *Acheron*. Likewise, the highly significant name Marcaciones Point he changed to the non-meaningful one of Flurry Point. Espinosa Point, Quintano Point, Port Pendulum, the Norte and Sur Channels were wiped altogether and the Cascada and Atlas Montanas weren't even considered. When it came to the name Grono Bay, Stokes was genuinely puzzled and concluding that it was a Spanish name, he spelt it Groznoz Bay instead. Also Mt Groznoz directly above the bay. Likewise with the name Thompson Sound he was equally baffled, and believing it to be named after Sir Edward Deas Thomson, the colonial secretary in New South Wales, he gave the names Deas Cove, Colonial Head and Secretary Island in Thompson Sound.

Some years ago the names Malaspina Reach, Pendulo Reach and Espinosa Point were restored on the map. Then in 1984 the author sent a submission to the New Zealand Geographic Board asking it to consider the restoration of the remainder of the Spanish names. Four of the names were eventually approved in 1987, Quintano Point, Cascada Bay, the highly significant name Marcaciones Point and the correction of the name Nea Islet to Nee Islets. But the names Norte and Sur Channels were rejected, it being pointed out that they were used as canoe passages by the early Maori and the names Te Awaatu

Entrance to Thompson Sound photographed from Deas Cove with Colonial Head, Secretary Island, on left. Names given by Captain Stokes in the mistaken belief that Thompson Sound was named after Deas Thomson, the colonial secretary. *(J. Hall-Jones)*

MARCACIONES
= POINT =
DON FELIPE BAUZA
OF THE SPANISH EXPEDITION
COMMANDED BY CAPTAIN MALASPINA
WAS THE FIRST EUROPEAN
TO EXPLORE DOUBTFUL SOUND.
HE LANDED ON THIS POINT
ON 25 FEBRUARY 1793

The plaque which was unveiled on Marcaciones Point in 1984. *(J. Hall-Jones)*

The *Renown* in Hall Arm with Spanish and New Zealand flags flying after the plaque unveiling in 1984. *(P. Hall-Jones)*

and Patea Channels were given instead. To confuse the issue these two narrow channels have long been known to fishermen as the Gut and Gaol Passage, so the names were added as alternative ones.

Marcaciones Point, the site of the first Spanish landing in New Zealand and Bauza's observation station for

The Spanish Ambassador, Dr Antonio Nunez, holding the Spanish flag at the bicentenary of the first Spanish landing in New Zealand on 25 February 1993. Marcaciones Point with plaque in background. Author on left. (*P. Hall-Jones*)

his first chart of Doubtful Sound, is obviously an important historic site. In recognition of this the author and Bart Porta, the Spanish Vice-Consul for New Zealand, mounted a plaque on the Point which was unveiled in 1984.

On 25 February 1993 Fiordland Travel Ltd organised a special excursion out to Marcaciones Point to celebrate the bicentenary of the Spanish exploration of Doubtful Sound. Dr Antonio Nunez, the Spanish Ambassador to Australia, graced the occasion by flying across from Canberra to participate in the event.

Bloodsucker's Sound

George Hansard, the erudite scribe of the *Acheron* Journal, gives us a delightful day-to-day account of the *Acheron's* survey of Doubtful Sound in 1851.

"The seas in this whole passage are unruffled as an inland lake", he writes. At times "the narrow passage contracted so much as to resemble a river" and the birds "which traversed from side to side seem greatly terrified at the strange apparition which invades their sequestered home".

The lack of wind inside the Sound brought out the sandflies, which were an "intolerable nuisance" to the surveyors working with their instruments. "It seems strange", meditates Hansard in his misery, "that the [sealers] who first explored the dark recesses of these [fjords] never hit upon such names as 'Bloodsucker's Sound', 'Venom Point' and 'Sandfly Bay'."

"Sailor [the ship's dog] has taken to climbing trees in his enthusiasm for catching birds, great or small. He bolts off suddenly in the night, captures a woodhen, returns and lays it before the tent floor, then settles himself down again to sleep. We almost live by that

"South Island Kiwi: Tokoeka". A drawing by someone, unknown, aboard the *Acheron*. (*National Maritime Museum*)

The great mass of Commander Peak at the entrance to Hall Arm. (*J. Hall-Jones*)

dog, says Bradshaw [the mate, after whom Bradshaw Sound was named] when away on duty in the bush. At nightfall there is a solemn silence. Presently there issues from the forest the Kiwi's note, first one, then another and another. Then a hoarse snorting announces the Kakapo, and presently numerous woodhens join in the cry. Grubs and worms form the food of the Kiwi, grass and herbage of the Kakapo, but the woodhen seems omnivorous; nothing comes amiss to him.

A very handsome Kakapo [captured no doubt by Sailor] was imprisoned in the ship's dispensary, through want of a proper cage. So long as daylight continued the animal remained stupid in a corner. But on the approach of night he became quite frisky, as all night birds invariably do. Clambering up among the jars and bottles on the shelves he bolted, or 'skoffed', some dozen pills for the inner man, flew through the skuttle and was drowned."

As the *Acheron* lay anchored in a cove (?Deas Cove) with "high precipices towering 5,000 feet above and the soundings giving 300 fathoms below" (a total of 7,000 fect) Hansard reflected on the great depth of these glacier-carved fjords. "What a dark and fearful gulf would be revealed to the eye were this and the other [fjords] suddenly laid dry."

From Thompson Sound the *Acheron* sailed five kilometres up the

Commander Peak framed in the Narrows of Hall Arm. (*J.Hall-Jones*)

The *Acheron* lying in Deas Cove, Thompson Sound, in 1851. Note the steep cliffs of Colonial Head, Secretary Island, on left of entrance. A drawing by Captain F. Evans. (*National Maritime Museum*)

Left: Commander George Richards (later Sir George) of the *Acheron* after whom Commander Peak was named. (*A. Day*)

Dr James Hector (later Sir James) who carried out a geological survey of the West Coast Fjords in 1863. (*Hocken Library*)

coast to the leg-shaped Nancy Sound, where the surveyors bestowed apt names such as Foot Arm, Heel and Toe Coves. The fjord was originally named by John Grono after one of his ships, the *Nancy*.

Frozen In

Dr James Hector, the provincial geologist, initially bypassed the entrance of Doubtful Sound on his survey of the coast in the yacht *Matilda Hayes* (Captain John Falconer) in 1863. But off the entrance to Nancy Sound the wind swung round to the north-west and they were blown back into Thompson Sound, where they sought anchorage in Deas Cove.

"We had hardly anchored", records Hector, "when the storm broke with great violence, the gusts of wind drawing through the narrow mountain valley having terrific force and accompanied by torrents of rain".

The storm continued for three days, then as the wind began to abate the yacht was allowed to drift down the Sound to "Doubtful Inlet", where "still led by the wind" they sailed up the "narrow and tortuous" Crooked Arm to its head. There, on the "extensive mud flats" of Haulashore Cove, they found "plenty of ducks and waterfowl". From the head of Haulashore Cove Hector walked across the low isthmus to Dagg Sound, now a 40 minute walk on a cut track.

(Dagg Sound was named after Captain William Dagg of the *Scorpion* which was sealing there in 1804. The *Acheron* struck a phenomenal downpour of rain while surveying Dagg Sound in 1851. "Within a few hours, no less than 14 magnificent cascades were pouring down the sides of the mountains around us, bringing with them trees of considerable size. The effect was as if a heavy

Crooked Arm frozen over in July. (*J. Hall-Jones*)

The yacht *Matilda Hayes* under tow in Lake McKerrow. (*Alexander Turnbull Library*)

Dagg Sound, from the exit of the short track from Crooked Arm, Doubtful Sound. (*J. Hall-Jones*)

Becalmed at the head of Crooked Arm, they began to tow the *Matilda Hayes* back down the Arm. By nightfall they were only halfway, anchored off a cove backed by "a precipitous cliff surmounted by little peaks". The scene inspired Hector's name of "Rampart Cove" for their anchorage. The next day they continued their slow progress, but eventually "a favourable breeze" carried them back to their old anchorage in Deas Cove. This time Hector was able to get ashore and his Maori guide, Henry Paramatta, took him to see "the swampy flat at the head of Deas Cove" where he and a party of whalers shot a takahe (notornis) in 1851. Interestingly, he also told Hector that "these birds are yet tolerably plentiful on the west side of the Te Anau Lake". (This would be Takahe Valley where the Maori hunted for takahe and where Dr G. Orbell rediscovered the bird in 1948.)

surf was breaking around the vessel. When the mist floated around our mastheads it produced a scene as grand as it is possible to conceive", records Commander Richards. "After two days of continual downpour the water alongside the vessel, which had been as salt as the ocean, became perfectly fresh".)

The *Matilda Hayes* lay in Haulashore Cove for a number of days, taking advantage of the beautiful, clear days that can often be experienced during the winter in the fjords. "We enjoyed a few days of magnificent weather, with sharp frosts towards day break, so that everything was covered with thick hoar frost." On 30 July the whole Sound was actually "covered with ice from side to side" and the *Matilda Hayes,* although moored in six fathoms of salt water, was frozen in. This unusual phenomenon of the Sound freezing over was due to there being a layer of "fresh water on the surface of the salt", as Hector explains.

Sunlit ramparts of Rampart Cove, Crooked Arm. (*P. McGahan*)

Notornis mantelli (takahe). Note colourful blue feathers, red bill and red legs. (*DOC*)

This second specimen of notornis was also procured by Walter Mantell who sent it to the British Museum, where it was mounted side by side with the first one. Like the remains of the dodo in the adjoining case, these only existing specimens of notornis attracted the daily attention of thousands of visitors. Although the original Dusky Sound specimen was retained by the British Museum, the second Deas Cove specimen was returned to New Zealand and presented to the National Museum in Wellington.

The Hermit of Doubtful Sound

Thanks to Robert Paulin we have a description of Percy Seymour BA, the school teacher – turned naturalist, who in 1887 opted out of his profession for a life of solitude in Doubtful Sound. Robert Paulin was aboard the *Stella* when she called at Percy Seymour's camp on Espinosa Point in the spring of 1887.

"We called on Mr Seymour, a gentleman who has determined to pass several years alone in this wild spot. He dwells by himself in a tent, with a dog or two, and is, I was told, studying the habits of the nocturnal birds of New Zealand, with the intention of writing a book about them. He had certainly chosen a romantic spot for his hermitage. His tent was pitched on the mainland [on Espinosa Point] by the shore of a little bay; Secretary Island, with its varied outline of wooded mountains, and an intervening mile of water, constituting a glorious frontispiece. Behind and on both sides of Mr Seymour's simple abode rose lofty green hills, and above them towered snow-covered peaks of giant proportions. A mountain torrent foamed into the little bay not many yards from his tent.

We arrived at the hermitage soon after sunrise one fine spring morning, and sent a boat off with stores for the hermit. He was an anxious-looking, middle-sized, middle-aged man. He said the rats on the mainland were destroying his stores, and accordingly he got the captain of the *Stella* to send a boat and shift his goods to a small island [Seymour Island] about two hundred yards from the shore. This island consisted of a few acres of rock covered with bush. Mr Seymour had a small boat of his own, and I fancy he was searching for gold or other minerals, for among the stores we landed for him was a digger's cradle. We waited three hours for him to finish his correspondence, which consisted of seventeen letters for all parts of the world, the captain having previously had instructions from the Government to give the hermit every assistance. After getting his letters we steamed away, leaving him to his own society for another three months.

This man was once a school-master, holding a good position and moving in first-class society. He has renounced all these advantages for this solemn, solitary existence. As we steamed away, I saw him standing watching us from the shore. A group of sailors were near me looking at his solitary figure. 'He won't see a soul for another three months now', said one, and then added reflectively and audibly 'poor devil', a verdict generally endorsed by his hearers. The study of birds may have taken him there; but there are those who think – if not insanity— it is love that has induced this voluntary banishment from the abodes of men."

Seymour Island, with Secretary Island in background. Photographed from Espinosa Point, where Percy Seymour originally camped. (*K. Morrison*)

For at least the next six months Percy Seymour continued happily in his lonely existence and in a letter (dated 30 March 1888) to Professor T. J. Parker of the Otago Museum he tells how he prefers "this life to teaching. With the exception of the first few weeks I have always extracted a certain amount of pleasure from it", he writes. "I am getting much stronger and acquiring a considerable share of physical vigour which makes me to a certain extent insensible to physical discomforts and keeps me in good spirits. I do not mind the solitude in the least. I do not remember being lonesome for a single day since I came. My dogs too are capital company. I have always some work on hand, or some plan to think out, to keep my thoughts occupied. I have now completed a large hut [on Seymour Island] and hope soon to occupy it which will largely diminish the discomforts due to the disgusting climate. Indeed as far as I am concerned I shall be quite content to live here and die here, only making enough to keep me going."

He then goes on to reveal that he was thinking of turning his hand to taxidermy to keep a little money coming in and that he had an agent in England who "does a good business in foreign skins". But "I want to practise on the larger and looser-feathered birds first and have not collected small birds as yet". Which was probably just as well, as he talks of being able to obtain South Island thrush and orange-wattled crows!

But when Robert Paulin called again in the spring of 1888 he found that "Mr Seymour had grown tired of playing the hermit in Doubtful Sound", had abandoned his plans of becoming a taxidermist there and had moved to the lighthouse settlement at Preservation Inlet, where gold had just been discovered. Bella Hislop in 1889 found that he was "living in a tiny house near the landing shed". Later he moved to the gold-mining town of Te Oneroa and took up teaching again, at the nearby Cromarty school.

In 1974 ranger Kim Morrison rediscovered the remains of Percy Seymour's hut on the tiny south-east point of Seymour Island, overlooking his dinghy harbour.

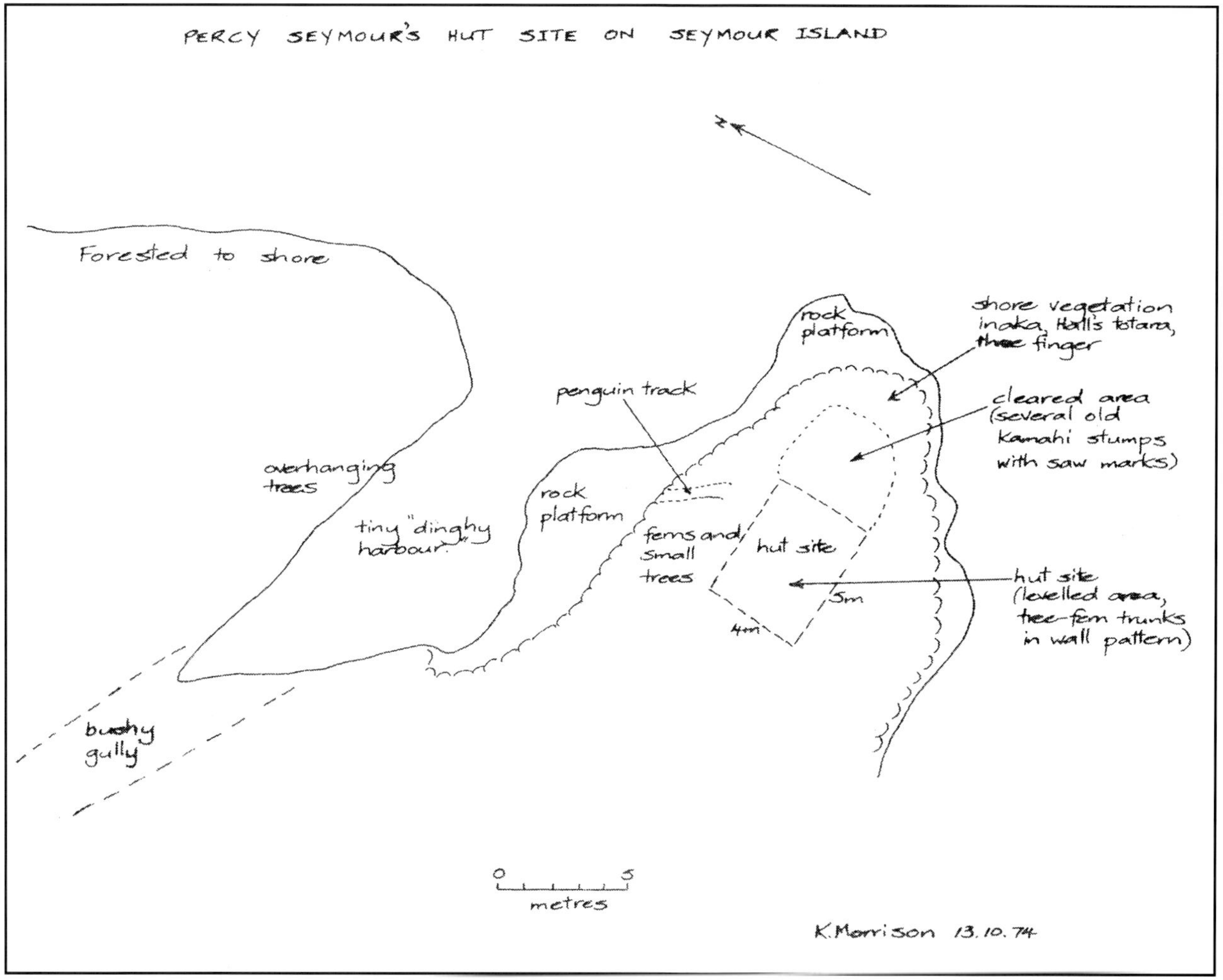

Diagram by Kim Morrison showing Percy Seymour's hut site and dinghy harbour on Seymour Island, 1974. (*K. Morrison*)

Wilmot Pass

In 1889 Professor Mainwaring Brown went missing while he and two companions were trying to find a route from the West Arm of Lake Manapouri through to Deep Cove at the head of Doubtful Sound. At least four searches were undertaken, but neither he nor his body were ever found.

Two of the searchers, Robert Murrell of Manapouri and John Barber, continued beyond Mainwaring Brown's camp in the Disaster Burn to cross the

Robert Murrell of Manapouri who crossed the Wilmot Pass twice in 1889, eight years before it was named. (*E. Hosken*)

Wilmot Pass (as yet unnamed) for the first time and become the first two Europeans to descend to Deep Cove.

On their ascent of Wilmot Pass from the Disaster Burn there was a "very dense fog obscuring all landmarks", records Murrell, "but trusting to the fog lifting later on we started down the saddle towards the coast. Our downward progress was interrupted by precipices of bare rock which necessitated our making detours to find places to descend them. After cutting down some branches that obstructed our view we saw a long silver-like streak far away down the valley. We gave vent to the first shout of joy that had ever been uttered in those wilds by any white man, because we were quite sure that the water we could see was Smith Sound [Malaspina Reach]." The sight gave "a fresh impetus to our feet" and they carried on down to Deep Cove. After making "a tour of the beach" and "inspecting the fine waterfall [Helena Falls] at the east end of the cove", they returned to their tent to find that it was "in possession of sandflies" and that the "bluebottles" had blown their blankets, even their tea bag and bread.

On 8 January they struggled back up onto the pass. This time the day was clear and they received their just reward. "Long we gazed down on the beautiful scene before us", records Murrell. "At our feet the valley was clothed in all the rich tints of the New Zealand forest, while around us arose high peaks covered in snow." Away below "lay Smith [Malapina] Sound like a wide silver ribbon". There should not be "the slightest difficulty in making a good road to Deep Cove", he prophesied.

Eight years later, in 1897, surveyor E. H. Wilmot stood on the same viewpoint and came to the same conclusion. The saddle provided "a good pass to Smith Sound which would be suitable for a road", he reported. Wilmot descended to Deep Cove and the pass was named Wilmot Pass.

On Wilmot's recommendation a tourist walking track was cut from the West Arm of Lake Manapouri to Deep Cove. In May 1900 C. W. Chamberlain, the Collector of Customs in Dunedin, walked the track while it was in the process of being constructed. Accompanied by Robert Murrell he came to a "very fine fall" where "the road party did me the honour to suggest that my name should be tacked to it, as I was their first visitor. But I compromised by giving them the name of my cottage in Dunedin, Cleve Garth, the meaning of which [hanging garden] just fits the situation. We found the road party's camp on the top of the pass, the tents nestled against the huge boulders which covered the top." As they descended towards Deep Cove they saw "the mountains

Wilmot Pass today, showing the road descending to Deep Cove. Mt Wilmot on right. (*J. Hall-Jones*)

Malaspina Reach from Wilmot Pass. End of the road and Manapouri tailrace at Deep Cove, directly below. Helena Falls on right. (*J. Hall-Jones*)

E. H. Wilmot who surveyed Wilmot Pass in 1897 and recommended it as a suitable route for a road. (*B. W. Hewat*)

between the sound and the sea, hazy and soft in the distance, a deep indigo purple in colour. The kakapos are very numerous. The road party found two that morning in broad daylight sitting in a fuschia wearing that embarrassed air of having been out all night, don't you know."

"We passed the road party halfway down to the sound and left our swags with them, to my great relief", he admits unashamedly. They finally reached the flat sandy beach of Deep Cove, "where a fine fall [Helena Falls] drops from a steep rocky face, not unlike the Stirling Fall at Milford Sound".

Unlike the Milford Track the Deep Cove Track never really took off and it slowly fell into neglect. Then, in 1921, Leslie Murrell of Manapouri obtained permission to reopen the track and build a hut at Deep Cove. Parties were guided over the track by Murrell who built a ladder on a steep pitch on the descent and this became known as "Leslie's Ladder". The Stella Burn (named after the ss *Stella* which took part in the search for Mainwaring Brown) was crossed on stepping stones and beyond that the track flattened out to reach the hut on the bank of the Lyvia River.

When functioning, which was not always the case, the launch *Constance* was available for cruises on the Sound. In 1954 Les Hutchins purchased the

The new lodge built at Deep Cove by Les Hutchins and the 're-engined' *Constance, 1955. (National Publicity Studio)*

estate of Leslie Murrell, 're-engined' the *Constance*, rebuilt the hut as a lodge, and this was the beginning of the giant tourist company, Fiordland Travel Ltd.

A Covered-in Town at Deep Cove

Six miles back in the mountains from Deep Cove, Lake Manapouri had long been recognised as having great potential for a hydro-electric power scheme. In the mid-1920s, when Wellington businessman Leigh Hunt was looking for a source of cheap hydro-electric power to establish a synthetic nitrate industry, Lake Manapouri seemed to provide the answer. With hydro-electric engineer Hugh Vickerman he mounted a "well-equipped expedition" to Doubtful Sound. They found that a "six and a half mile" tunnel under the mountains from the West Arm of Lake Manapouri to Deep Cove would give a fall of "540 feet" to a powerhouse constructed at Deep Cove.

"A town large enough to accommodate 2,000 people" to service the nitrate factory and power plant would be built at Deep Cove and with the heavy rainfall of the area "the streets and playing areas would need to be covered in". With 80 fathoms of water at Deep Cove, a cantilever wharf would enable the largest of ships to berth, so that the nitrates could be exported directly from the factory.

A company was formed in 1926 and with an eye to publicity for overseas investors a photographer,

From left, Hugh Vickerman, Sir Douglas Mawson and Leigh Hunt. Photographed in 1928 during their investigation of Doubtful Sound for a hydro-electric power scheme for a nitrate industry. (*A. Leigh Hunt*)

Right: The Helena Falls, where photographer Barton dangled precariously from a rope trying to film the falls. End of Manapouri tailrace in foreground. (*J. Hall-Jones*)

"Barton" (?Burton of the famous Burton Bros) was asked to photograph the scenery of the Sound.

"Barton's outstanding feat took place at the top of the Helena Falls", records Hunt, "where it spills over the 800-foot cliff at an angle of 70 degrees. Our photographer's ambition was to get a close-up movie of the fall in its full glory about fifty feet below the spillway. As he sat in a loop of a long, stout rope we lowered him down until he signalled to stop. But fate was cruelly against him. Before he could even get his camera adjusted he started to spin round, round and round, faster and faster. It made us giddy to watch him from our firm stand on the cliff edge. What pangs of vertigo

tortured poor Barton he alone knows. After a time the spinning grew slower and slower and then stopped, but, alas, before the artist could take even a single shot he started spinning again, this time in the reverse rotation. This occurred time after time. Thus he dangled in mid-air with some 500 feet of space beneath him and with the majesty of his quest going to waste but a few feet distant from him. It must have been fully half an hour, during which time he was nearly eaten alive by sandflies, before Barton, acknowledging his utter defeat, signalled us to haul him up. However, through Barton we obtained nearly one thousand feet of film of glorious scenery which provided valuable

The *Wanganella* moored in Deep Cove, where it acted as a floating hostel for men working on the tailrace tunnel and Wilmot Pass road. (G. *Howard*)

The blast from the final breakthrough of the first tailrace tunnel lifts the hard-hats of the workers and Ralph Hanan M.P. (in foreground), 1968. (*G. Howard*)

publicity for the company."

Professor Sir Douglas Mawson, the eminent Australian geologist and Antarctic explorer, was invited to inspect the proposed scheme. During 1928 Mawson spent several weeks in "the fastness of Doubtful Sound" and according to Hunt, "he was more than satisfied with his investigations". Mawson proceeded to London where he was able to obtain an offer to underwrite a flotation of $13,000,000. Triumphantly Hunt showed the cable to Prime Minister Joseph Coates, who agreed to present a bill "first thing next session to enable the company to secure this fine offer". But two months later Coates' party was voted out of office and the new premier, Sir Joseph Ward, refused to endorse the proposal. The "covered-in town" at Deep Cove, with its population of 2,000 never eventuated and the whole idea of a power scheme lay dormant for another 30 years.

During the early 1960s Comalco was looking for a source of cheap, continuous electricity for the production of aluminium at a smelter to be built at Bluff. The Government agreed to construct an underground powerhouse at West Arm with a six mile tailrace tunnel under the mountains to exit at Deep Cove. A 12 mile road was to be constructed over the Wilmot Pass to allow the heavy equipment for the powerhouse to be brought into Deep Cove by ship and transported over to West Arm. In 1963 the former trans-Tasman liner *Wanganella* was moored at Deep Cove as a floating hostel for the men working on the tailrace tunnel and the Wilmot Pass road.

Below: By way of contrast the huge rock-boring machine emerges slowly, like some primeval monster, at the breakthrough of the second tailrace in 2001. (*B. Leith*)

The Outdoor Education Centre at Deep Cove. (*J. Hall-Jones*)

So the Manapouri power scheme finally eventuated, with a powerhouse at Manapouri and not Doubtful Sound, as envisaged by Hunt, and for the production of aluminium not nitrates. The factory was at Bluff, not Doubtful Sound and the "floating village" of the *Wanganella* was only a temporary one, and not a permanent "covered-in town" of 2,000. Forty years later when a second tailrace tunnel became necessary, it was constructed by a huge rock-boring machine, and not by rock-blasting, as with the first.

As an end-result of this huge project, the Wilmot Pass road has been left as an access road to Doubtful Sound for tourists and fishermen, and Deep Cove has gained a fine Outdoor Centre for the school children of Southland.

CHAPTER 4

Milford Haven

Milford Sound is the most remarkable harbour yet visited by the Acheron in New Zealand.
George Hansard, 1851

In his scholarly *Journal of the Acheron* George Hansard gives us a graphic account of the *Acheron's* entry into Milford Sound, referring to it as "the most remarkable harbour yet visited by the *Acheron* in New Zealand".

"On 7 March 1851, having remained in Bligh's [Bligh Sound] one day we started for Milford Haven northwards. The day was superb and after sailing along a precipitous wooded shore we came in sight of our destination about 3 pm.

Here in remarkable contrast to the general character of New Zealand scenery, the vast precipices enclosing the outer basin are treeless; indeed nearly bare of any verdue of any kind. As the *Acheron* steamed slowly to her anchorage beneath these cliffs, towering several thousand feet on either [side], her masts seemed to dwindle into nothing. From the insignificance [of the *Acheron*] we were able to more fully comprehend the vast elevation of the snow capped summits [above]. [See cover painting.]

The haven sometimes expands into a broad sheet of water, then sometimes contracts [at The Narrows] so as to [restrict the view ahead]. It has two considerable falls of water [the Stirling and Bowen Falls] which precipitate themselves into the sea like fine wreaths of snow.

It was a most lovely day, warm and sunlit,

The same view as the sketch of the Bowen Falls *(facing page)* today. *(J. Hall-Jones)*

Sketch of the Bowen Falls by Captain Evans. (*British Maritime Museum*)

with a deep blue sky above us. As the ship came abreast of the first cataract [the Stirling Falls], the brilliant sunbeams refracted in the spray, which rose in clouds from its base showing all the rainbow's prismatic colours. Just opposite, we stopped for soundings and found no bottom at more than 200 fathoms.

The *Acheron* dropped the anchor immediately abreast a second fall [Bowen Falls], ascertained to have a descent of 200 feet. The violent rain of the preceding days had greatly augmented the volume of its water which seemed to burst from a large reservoir with an incessant roar. [A roar] which was heard with additional solemnity during the stillness of the night.

Next day the ship was moved into the furthermost anchorage [Deepwater Basin] where she was landlocked. Owing to the rivers and cascades discharging here, the water is nearly fresh alongside.

A pointed mountain of naked rock 5,000 feet high [Mitre Peak] encloses us on one hand. A still more elevated mountain of 6,700 feet, clothed with rich verdue below but equally bare on its summit, seems impending over the vessel on the NE. And a savage

Sketch of the Stirling Falls by Captain Frederick Evans of the *Acheron*. (*British Maritime Museum*)

looking gorge, down which a brawling torrent rushes, flows over the shingly beach into the sea [the Cleddau River].

These then are the chief features of this, the most remarkable harbour yet visited by the *Acheron* in New Zealand."

Captain Frederick Evans and Commander George Richards were equally captivated by "this most remarkable harbour", Captain Evans painting the majestic scenery and Commander Richards describing it. A magnificent painting by Captain Evans shows the little wooden paddle-steamer, rigged as a barque, anchored in Freshwater Basin, close to the Bowen Falls. In the centre of the painting is the great glacier dome of the "perpetually snow-capped" Pembroke Peak, soaring high above Harrison Cove. To the left in the painting is "the remarkable shaped Mitre, rising abruptly to 5,560 feet from the sea, perhaps the most striking feature of the whole sound". Opposite Mitre Peak are the Stirling Falls, the "first waterfall" that the *Acheron* passed on her way into the fjord. Leading back from the Stirling Falls is the "dome-shaped" Lion.

"The pointed mountain of naked rock" which Stokes named Mitre Peak, after a bishop's mitre. (*J. Hall-Jones*)

Above right: Captain Frederick Evans (later Sir Frederick, the Hydrographer) who made several sketches and paintings of Milford Sound in 1851. (*A. Day*)

Right: Captain Evans' painting from the head of the Sound showing the principal features of Milford Sound. *HMS Acheron* anchored near the Bowen Falls on right. (*Alexander Turnbull Library*)

Comparing Milford Sound with all the other sounds they had surveyed, Commander Richards considered Milford, although shorter than most, "far surpasses them all" for its "remarkable features and magnificent scenery. Its narrow entrance, with its stupendous cliffs which rise perpendicularly as a wall from the water's edge to a height of several thousand feet, invest Milford Sound with a character of solemnity and grandeur which description can barely realise."

The *Acheron* made to depart from Milford Sound on 13 March but was detained for a week in Anita Bay at the entrance by adverse weather. "By anchoring half a cable off shore and hauling close in with hawsers fast to the trees the *Acheron* found considerable shelter. Much of the greenstone lying about the beach [of Anita Bay]", writes Hansard "was an inferior type called Takawai which for the most part is little esteemed by the Maori [for tools]. Of [this] fine rich green and semi-transparent kind, most of their personal ornaments were formed."

The Welsh Connection

Interestingly, George Hansard uses the term "Milford Haven" twice in his journal. One of the *Acheron's* surveyors, W. J. W. Hamilton, also uses the term on his sketch of the "Land to the Northward of Milford Haven". Captain Stokes had Edward Meurant's early sealing map with him and this gives the sealers' original name "Milford Haven".

With all this prior use of the name "Milford Haven" by the early sealers and

The great fortress of Pembroke Castle, Milford Haven, Pembrokeshire. (*J. Hall-Jones*)

Below: The great glaciated dome of Mt Pembroke in Milford Sound. (*J. Hall-Jones*)

Captain John Lort Stokes of *HMS Acheron* who, like the original namer John Grono, also came from Milford Haven, Wales. (*National Library of Australia*)

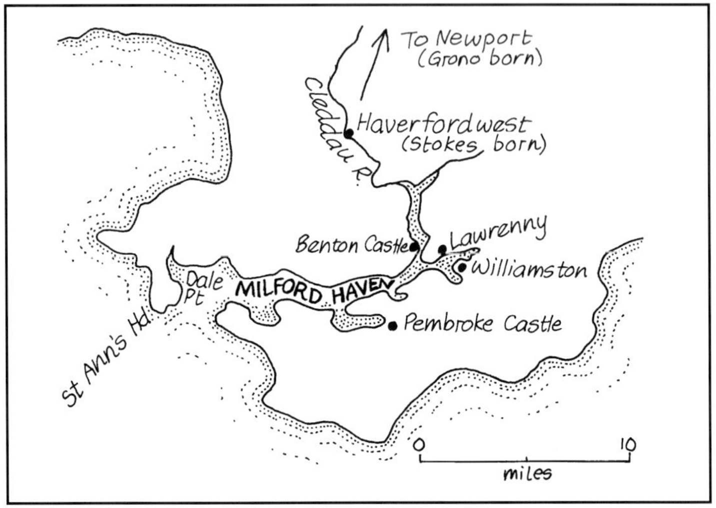

Diagram showing the origin of the Milford Sound names that Stokes took from Milford Haven in Wales. (*Copyright J. Hall-Jones*)

Left: The *Acheron* chart of Milford Sound showing the names that Stokes gave in 1851. (*Alexander Turnbull Library*)

some of his officers, Stokes, who by an extraordinary coincidence actually came from Milford Haven in Wales, had a wonderful opportunity to perpetuate the name of his homeland on the map of New Zealand. Instead he chose differently and changed it to Milford Sound. A pity, because if he really wanted to change the name, Milford Fjord would have been a better choice, it being a glacier-carved fjord and not a river-formed sound.

Perhaps Stokes thought it 'improper' to name the sound after the Welsh haven, as the following comment suggests:- "The Welshman who first penetrated into this deep inlet seems to have retained but an imperfect recollection of the celebrated haven of his native land after which he thought proper to name it." Be this as it may, Stokes was still puzzled as to who the early Welshman was that bestowed the original name. He was not to know that it was the same Captain John Grono of "Gronow's" and "Thompson's" in Doubtful Sound who named it after his homeland in Pembrokeshire. John Grono was born at Newport, only a few kilometres north of Milford Haven. In 1798 he worked his way out to New South Wales where he established a successful shipbuilding yard on the Hawkesbury River. From 1809 until 1824 he ventured across to the Fiordland coast on sealing expeditions naming a number of the fjords, including Milford Haven, in the process. He even supplied information for the "sailing directions" for Milford Haven, advising Anita Bay (then unnamed) as "the most suitable position" to anchor at the entrance. Here "the forest spars are of excellent quality and in abundance; and enormous mountain ranges covered with perpetual snows can be seen in the interior".

Although Stokes chose not to use Grono's name of Milford Haven on his chart he decided to continue the association by bestowing place-names taken from the Welsh haven. Stokes lived at Haverfordwest, just 7 kilometres up the Cleddau River from Milford Haven, and he was thoroughly familiar with the names that he gave from his home haven. These include: Cleddau River, Pembroke Peak (after Pembroke Castle), Benton Peak (after Benton Castle), Llawrenny Peaks (after Lawrenny village), Dale Point and St Ann's Point (both at the entrance of the Welsh haven), and Williamston Point (after Williamston village). His name Harrison Cove was probably given as a tribute to John Harrison, the inventor of the Harrison clock which they were using to measure longitude.

John Boultbee

Prior to the *Acheron* survey, the sealer John Boultbee also used the name "Milford Haven" in his journal in 1826. Boultbee's sealing gang had a "crazy hut" at Anita Bay and Boultbee records how he and his mates hauled their boat out on the beach and slept the night in the hut.

"Milford Haven", writes Boultbee, using the sealers name for the sound, "is a wild romantic looking place, abounding in high mountains and intermediate deep vallies. The woods are abundantly supplied with game [such] as woodhens [wekas], green birds [kakapo], emus [the larger species of kiwi] etc.

On the left side of this place [he was coming from the north] is a deep and narrow passage [The Narrows] between two tiers of mountains which we called the flue, through which the wind blows at times with great violence." A dramatic first description of the wind-prone Narrows of Milford Sound.

The Hermit of Milford Sound

On 1 December 1877 Donald Sutherland arrived at the head of Milford Sound in his small open boat, the *Porpoise,* with only a dog for a companion. He had set out from Thompson Sound that morning and sailed the distance of 100 miles in 10 hours. With justification he wrote: "I don't want to sound my own trumpet too much, but this is a bully run for a man in an open boat in 10 hours."

Sutherland remained there for eight days, exploring the lower Arthur River and then continued on to Jackson's Bay. A few weeks later (in early 1878) he was back and began building a slab hut on a rocky shelf of land in Freshwater Basin (in the vicinity of the present Tourist Centre).

The "Esperance Chalet" as he grandly named his slab hut with its thatched roof was just above the shoreline with a seawall of rocks in front. By 1897 he had built two similar huts a little up the hillside behind, the upper one also of slab timber, the middle one of pungas, both with thatched roofs. Each hut had its own paper and mail box for the three-monthly delivery service by the *ss Stella.* 'Streets' were 'laid out' and later he extended the "Esperance Chalet" by adding a verandah, a corrugated iron roof and another room. A flagmast was erected and a stone pier built out from the waterfront.

Anita Bay at the entrance to Milford Sound where John Boultbee's sealing gang once had a "crazy hut". (*J. Hall-Jones*)

Donald Sutherland standing above his three thatched huts at the "City of Milford". (*Burton Bros*)

With all these major works going on the settlement had obviously reached urban status and quite rightly it became known as the "City of Milford". Truly great things were expected of it!

In 1889 Sutherland was visited by Robert Paulin, who leaves us an interesting description of the hermit, the "City" and the Sound.

> "The house stands about 100 yards from the water and is made of wood. It is well and strongly built and has three rooms. The outer door was open and we went in. We found everything very clean and neat [inside with] wood laid in the fireplace and many objects of interest arranged tastefully about the room. On a table were several letters for the government steamer [*ss Stella*]. Behind the dwelling were some outhouses, one of which was fitted up for a forge and contained a large and good collection of tools, well kept. On a carpenter's bench was a diary evidently meant to be seen, and it was perused by some of the men.
>
> There was a small garden at the back of the house, [but] it struggled for existence with a mass of weeds and young native growth. Also roses, rhubarb, peas and strawberry plants, the latter had a good show of fruit not yct ripc. I wcnt for a ramble through the bush [behind] where I got a good look at a saddle-bird [saddleback, now extinct on the mainland], a beautiful, reddish-brown bird with a dark bar across its back and with red wattles."

Later he met Sutherland who he describes as "tall, heavily built, with a fresh complexion and bright blue eyes. That Sutherland is a man of taste is evident to anyone who has been in his house."

In an interesting comment on Sutherland's explorations of the area Paulin writes:

"His surveys of the district show considerable ability in one who has not been trained in this work. I have no doubt", continues Paulin, "that before long there will be an hotel at the head of the sound, somewhere near where Sutherland himself is. Sutherland will most likely be the landlord with boats and guides to the mountains. Tourists will come to far-famed Milford Sound in large numbers [to see] one of the wonders of New Zealand", he prophesied.

"From our anchorage [off Sutherland's house] we were encircled by views; any one of which would suffice in Europe or America to attract crowds of tourists annually to the spot. The remarkable outline of Mitre Peak, the most strikingly shaped mountain in New Zealand; the majesty of the Bowen Falls, a vibrating, foaming pillar of water; the towering rock face of the Sheerdown Cliffs; the [great glaciated dome] of Pembroke rising majestically from the sea."

At the time of Paulin's prophecies, the Milford Track had been discovered only a few months previously and still had to be developed. The road to Milford Sound was 60 years away and aeroplanes hadn't even been invented. The only easy access to Milford Sound was by cruise boat, albeit at considerable expense.

The "City of Milford" in 1887. The lowest of the three huts, the "Esperance Chalet", has been renovated by adding a verandah and replacing the thatched roof with corrugated iron. Note flagmast and stone pier. Sutherland is standing in the dinghy. (*Burton Bros*)

CHAPTER 5

Sutherland's Sound

Landing at Little Bay I entered a tidal river which I determined to follow up as far as I could with the boat.
Donald Sutherland, 1883

The *Acheron* surveyors missed the entrance to Sutherland Sound as they sailed up from Bligh Sound, "a little more than a mile off shore". All they saw was a long line of sand-dunes at the head of an open bay, which they called "Little Bay" on their chart.

But the early sealers knew of Sutherland Sound and called it "Little Bligh Sound", because of its close proximity to Bligh Sound. The Maori had an even better name for it, "Hapua", recognising it simply as a sea "lagoon". Notwithstanding, Donald Sutherland's name is rightly linked to Sutherland Sound, because he both charted it and described it in great detail when he rediscovered the Sound in 1883.

The wall of golden sand-dunes at the head of "Little Bay", which conceals the entrance to Sutherland Sound. (*J. Hall-Jones*)

The long, narrow entrance channel behind the sand-dunes. (*D. Kraft*)

The shallow entrance bar at the south end of the sandpit. (*J. Hall-Jones*)

Sutherland's Chart

In 1883 Donald Sutherland set out from the "City of Milford" in his open sailing boat, *Porpoise,* to explore the coastline south of Milford Sound. At the same time the prospector was always keeping an eye out for minerals, asbestos, 'rubies' (garnets) and of course there was always the hope of finding gold. After landing at Poison Bay he continued "five miles to the southward to land at Little Bay". Crossing a bar "3 fathoms deep at low water" at the south end of the sandy beach, "I entered a tidal river which I determined to follow up as far as I could with the boat". Once inside the bar the tidal river became deeper and maintained its width for "a distance of $1\frac{1}{2}$ miles beyond which it expands into a saltwater lake, 6 miles long and 1 mile wide. The lower part of this lake is a shingle [bank], dry at low tide", he reported. "In the upper part of the lake the depth is considerable, some 20 fathoms." (His chart shows a maximum sounding of 32 fathoms.)

Proceeding to the head of the "saltwater lake" Sutherland noted that it "narrowed to half its width to receive two rivers coming from the NE and SE respectively", with a delta in between. The smaller river running from the NE lay on the northern, sunny side of the "Rugged Mts" dividing the two valleys and Sutherland called it the Light River. The larger river on the southern, shaded side issued from "a tremendous ravine whose vertical

The explorer Donald Sutherland who rediscovered and charted Sutherland Sound in 1883. Photograph by Norman Deck in 1911. (*Courtesy George R. Chance collection*)

The head of Sutherland Sound, showing the gorge of the Dark River straight ahead and the Light River Valley leading off to the left. The sunlit "Rugged Mts" in between. (*J. Hall-Jones*)

eyes of sharks watching him closely, ever hopeful of picking up scraps or perhaps something larger than that!)

"The land between the lake and the sea is heavily timbered", Sutherland observed, "and abounding in bird life. Wekas are especially abundant; scarcely less so are pigeons, kakas, kiwis, kakapos and roas [large kiwis]. Redbills and penguins are in great numbers on the shingle [bank] when the tide is out."

Sutherland passed on his detailed findings and chart to the government geologist Alexander McKay, who felt that they were worthy of publication and proceeded to do so. Commenting on Sutherland's observations, McKay pointed out that Sutherland Sound is a "lesser [fjord] than Milford Sound because it was excavated by less extensive snowfields than the great glacier of Milford Sound. Although the saltwater lake inland from Little Bay is still a [fjord], owing to its greater depth and length", it is in the process of filling in and forming flat land fit for settlement. Confirming McKay's comment, Sutherland's map of 1883 shows the lower shingle bank portion of his "saltwater lake" forming just a third of the fjord, whereas today the bank has backfilled to more than half the length of the fjord. In other words Sutherland Sound is a 'dying' fjord in the process of becoming a lake. The ultimate example of this closing off process is Lake McKerrow, where the tidal Hollyford River now runs through the reclaimed settlement land of Martins Bay.

During 2001 my German kayaking mate, Dieter Kraft and I seakayaked round the whole shoreline of Sutherland Sound. Entering the dark peat-stained waters of the large Dark River we paddled up to where a waterfall tumbles

sides rise to a height of 1,500 feet" and he named it the Dark River. The "Caithness Mts" on the south side of Sutherland Sound he named after his home county in Scotland.

"The lake abounds with fish", he observed, "and following them is no scarcity of sharks, which infest the tidal river and lake wherever fish are found". (Float-plane pilot Chris Willet informs me that while floundering in Sutherland Sound some years ago the light from his torch lit up the hungry

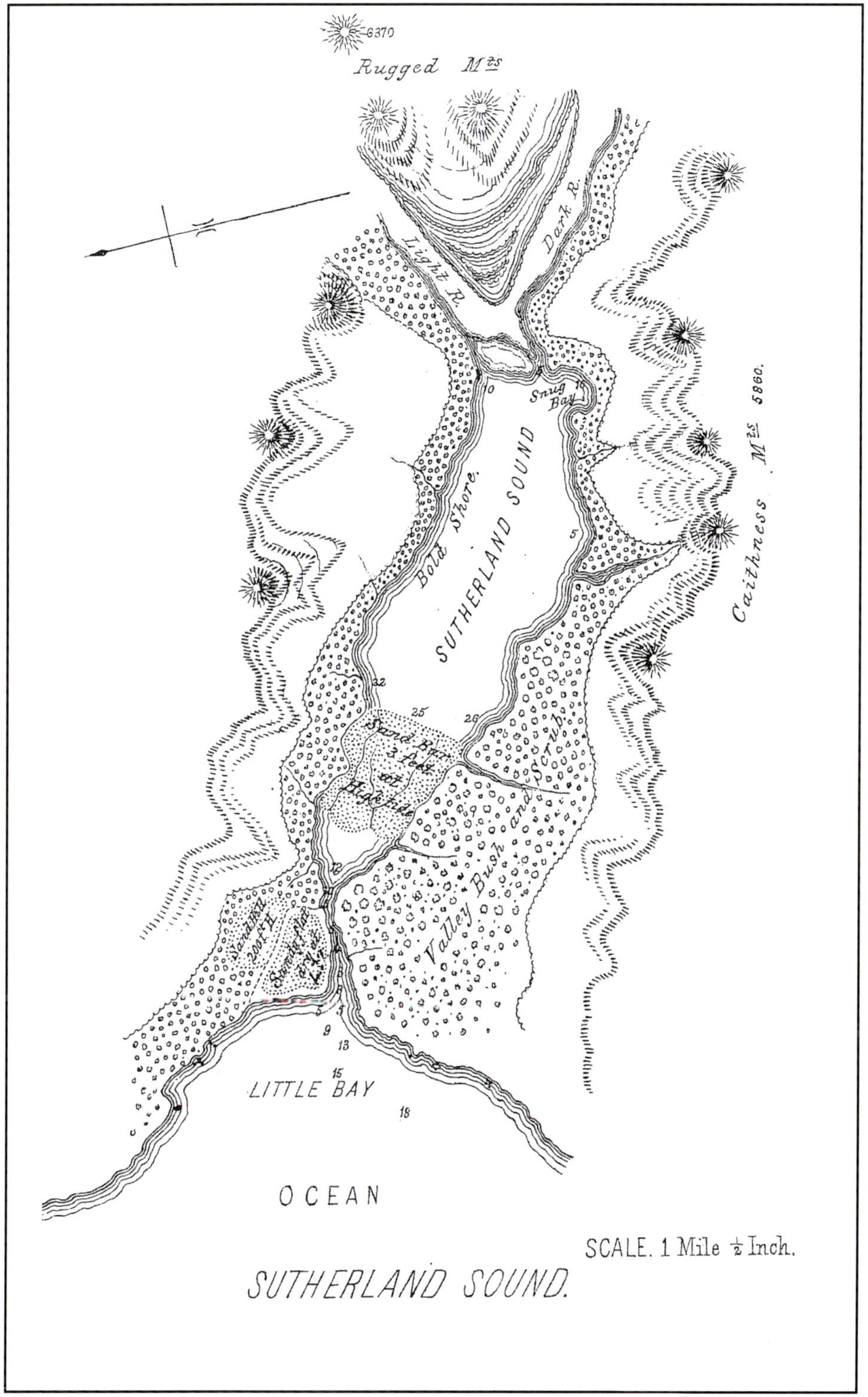

Right: Painting of South Island kiwis by John Buchanan, 1863. (*Friends of the Turnbull Library*)

Left: Sutherland's map of Sutherland Sound, 1883. (*Trans. N.Z. Institute*)

Below: The golden pingoa grass that covers the sand-dunes on the sandspit. (*J. Hall-Jones*)

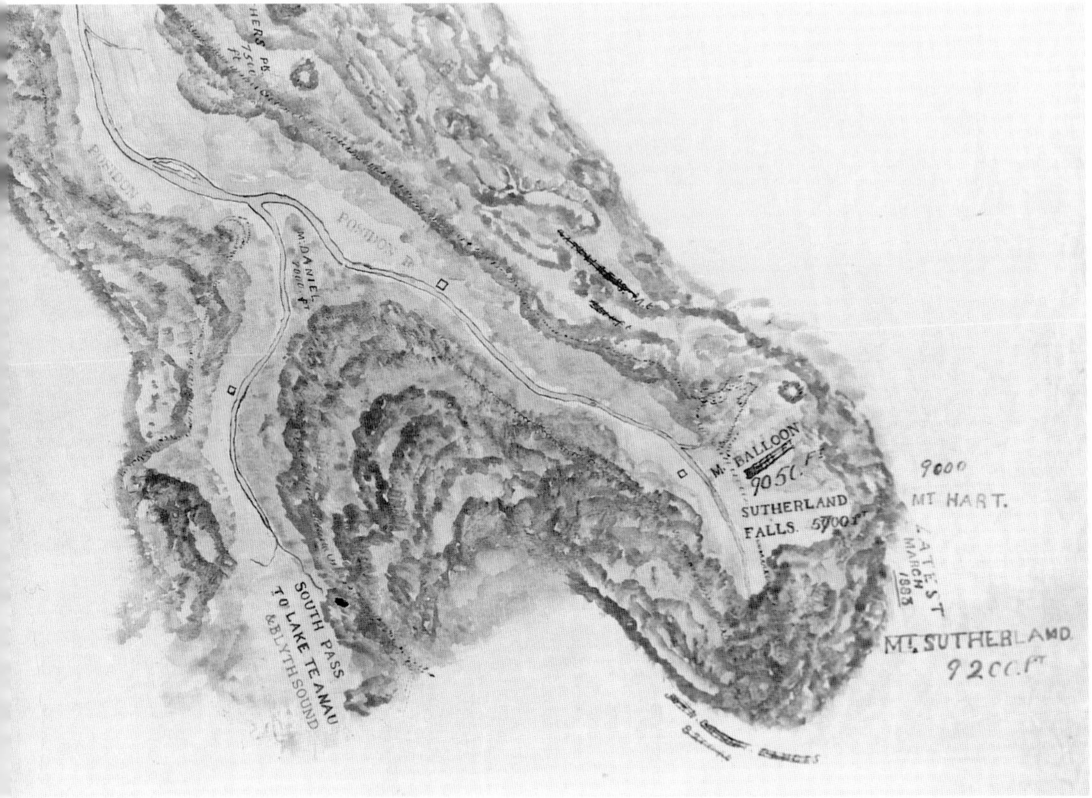

Sutherland's map of the head of the Arthur River Valley, 1880, showing his "South Pass to Lake Te Anau and Blyth Sound". Also the Sutherland Falls. (*Mrs A. S. Rose, Hocken Library*)

down the "tremendous ravine" from Lake Grave. Returning down-river we found that we were unable to enter the Light River, so we stood off the two valleys in our kayak, contrasting the sunlit Light River Valley with the gloomy, foreboding Dark River Valley. The tide was out, revealing the extensive estuarine mudflats of the Sound, but we were able to paddle down a sinuous channel to the sandspit at the entrance. Landing on the sandspit we wandered through Sutherland's "200 foot high" (a generous figure) black sand-dunes, beautifully crowned with golden pingoa grass. Crossing the tidal river at the entrance of the Sound, which Sutherland records as "running at 5 knots", we camped for the night inside the bar. The morning dawned with a calm Tasman Sea outside, so we crossed the bar at the turn of the high tide and beat it down to Bligh Sound as fast as our paddles could paddle!

Light River Valley

Prior to rediscovering Sutherland Sound, Sutherland explored the Arthur River Valley in 1880 where he discovered a pass, "South Pass", which he notes on his map as leading through "To Lake Te Anau and Blyth Sound" (Bligh Sound). Although Sutherland was not to know the valley that he saw on the far side of his "South Pass" was the Light River Valley leading down to his Sutherland Sound, not Bligh Sound.

In 1959 Alister McDonald's party traversed a saddle 3 kilometres south of Sutherland's "South Pass" to become the first party to descend the Light River Valley to Sutherland Sound.

Dark River Valley

In 1905 the famous Fiordland explorer W. G. ("Bill") Grave and his party arrived out at the head of Sutherland Sound, having skirted around Sutherland's "tremendous ravine" of the Dark River and the high bluffs of Lake Grave behind. Grave had set out from the Worsley Arm of Lake Te Anau. with three companions, Thomas (later Sir Thomas) Hunter, Alfred ("Gulliver") Grenfell and B. ("Sumor") Smith. After crossing the icy and precipitous Hunter Pass ("the Devil's own pass" as they called it later) they descended the Dark River Valley to Lake Grave. At first they thought that this "large sheet of water" was Sutherland Sound. But when their "aneroid registered 300 feet above sea level" and they found "no evidence of a tide", they realised that they had arrived at a large lake instead. After climbing over the high bluffs that rise straight from the edge of Lake Grave, they obtained their first view of Sutherland Sound. But their way was blocked by "a narrow gorge" (Sutherland's ravine). Backtracking round the gorge they descended to the mouth of the Dark River, where they camped for the night.

"Sutherland Sound is rarely visited because of a bar at its mouth", comments Grave, "and although it does not compare with Milford, it is much finer than Bligh Sound". (At Bligh Sound Grave's party had camped at the very head of the fjord and could not see the magnificent lofty peaks of the main sound.)

"We spent the morning of a beautiful day fishing [in the fjord]", recounts Grave, "and in the afternoon, having only two days' provisions left, we started on the return journey. We had taken three weeks on the outward journey and knew that we must now depend entirely on the gun, or starve." Grave's worst fears were to come true as they ascended Starvation Creek to Hunter Pass. For the first day a spoonful of dried apples was all that each man had to eat, the next day a spoonful of dried milk was the ration and on the third a spoonful of cocoa. In desperation they gnawed at the flax-like leaves of astelia, but found them very bitter. Then on the evening of their third day of starvation "we heard

Left: The gorge of the Dark River through which Grave's party descended from Lake Grave to the head of Sutherland Sound. (*J. Hall-Jones*)

Below: Members of Grave's expedition to Sutherland Sound in 1905. From left: (Sir) Thomas Hunter, Alfred ("Gulliver") Grenfell and W. G. ("Bill") Grave. (*A.C. Gifford*)

a weka clucking near the tent. I trembled so much in fear that I should miss it", relates Grave, "that I could hardly take aim. It fell. We were not long getting the fire going. A few minutes later, a kea, perhaps attracted by the unexpected sight of smoke, drew near. In no time it was in company with the weka in the billy. We were saved!"

Arriving back at Worsley Arm they were picked up by the lake steamer. It was only when they compared themselves with the passengers that they realised what a serious state of malnutrition they were in.

CHAPTER 6

The Wild Natives of Bligh Sound

The people belong to a small, isolated tribe and are known as the wild men of the mountains.
Capt. J. L. Stokes, 1851

The Hawkesbury River, N.S.W., where Governor Bligh had a farm right next door to Grono's farm and shipyard (on the near bank), where Grono built the *Governor Bligh*. (*Mitchell Library*)

Known as "Bligh's" to the early sealers, Bligh Sound was yet another name bestowed by John Grono, after his first sealing ship, the *Governor Bligh*. Once again Captain Stokes was baffled by the origin of a name on Meurant's chart and believing that the famous Captain Bligh of the "Mutiny of the Bounty" fame had actually visited Bligh Sound, Stokes added the names Bounty Haven and Mutiny Peak to features of the Sound.

The reason for Grono naming Bligh Sound ran deeper than simply the name of his sealing vessel. After Captain William Bligh was deposed as Governor of New South Wales he acquired a farm right next door to Grono's farm and shipbuilding yard on the Hawkesbury River. So when Grono built his first sealing ship in 1809 he named it after his distinguished neighbour, who was well liked on the Hawkesbury.

So much for the European name of the Sound. To the Maori it was known as Hawea, because after the massacre of the Hawea by the Ngaitahu at Preservation Inlet in 1780

The great overhanging seacliff where Paddy Gilroy saw smoke issuing from the "Cave of the Hawea" in 1842. (*J. Hall-Jones*)

(see next chapter) the few survivors fled to Bligh Sound, where they became known as the "Wild Natives" or "Lost Tribe" of Fiordland.

The Cave of the Hawea

In 1842 Paddy Gilroy, the legendary skipper of the *Amazon,* sailed into Bligh Sound on a sealing expedition. As they entered the fjord the sealers were surprised to see smoke issuing from a great seacliff straight ahead, at the base of Mt Alarm. Mooring their ship at the foot of the overhanging cliff, they landed on a rocky shelf and scrambled up a few metres to discover a "cave", really an overhang, beneath the bluff. The floor was divided into two sections, an inner bone-dry area where "places had been scooped out of the soft sandstone for sleeping", and an outer cooking area.

The arrival of the sealers had interrupted the cooking operations of the occupants and the frightened cave-dwellers had fled along "a well-defined

Paddy Gilroy, the legendary sealer and whaler, skipper of the *Amazon*. (*M. G Skerrett*)

track" to the high country above. Three Maori members of Paddy Gilroy's crew gave chase to them as high as the snowline. Their "tracks were easy to follow in the snow", they reported, but they never caught up with the fugitives. As the pursuers were Ngaitahu the Hawea had good reason to be afraid and flee, as they believed that their lives were in danger.

Returning to the "Cave of the Hawea", as it became known, Gilroy's men left intact the Hawea's "fishing lines and some flax baskets in the process of being woven". But they brought away "a whalebone mere and a flax mat". After this encounter with the frightened fugitives the mountain above the "Cave of the Hawea" became known as Alarm Mountain and the bay as Escape Cove.

Gilroy carried on with his business of slaughtering seals in the Sound, using Amazon Cove as an overnight anchorage. An Irishman living in Bluff, Gilroy is described as a "queer little figure of a man, short and tubby, with a

Our precarious landing at the "Cave of the Hawea". (*J. Hall-Jones*)

Mystic valley of the Wild Natives River. Sunlit mudflats at the mouth of the river at the head of Bligh Sound. (*J. Hall-Jones*)

brogue as thick as pea-soup. Overflowing with kindness and good temper, his ship was a veritable ark of refuge for any unfortunate who needed help. His men adored him and believed him capable of anything."

In 2001, as Dieter and I paddled down the coast from Sutherland Sound to Bligh Sound we were both hoping to rediscover the "Cave of the Hawea". Rounding the rocky point at the entrance to Bligh Sound we could see in the distance, dead ahead, a white seacliff, the perfect lookout for a frightened tribe in fear of pursuit. As we drew nearer to the white cliff, a huge overhanging bluff appeared from behind the tip of Turn Round Point, with Mt Alarm looming high above. A tiny rocky inlet led into the foot of the bluff and landing with some difficulty we took turns to scramble up through the boulders to examine the foot of the great cliff. There, close beneath the huge overhang, was the innermost bone-dry floor of soft sandstone for sleeping. On the outermost side was the cooking area, with many fragments of charcoal and burnt shells scattered along in the line of the overhang. A short distance away from the landing was the stony beach of Escape Cove, where there was a permanent

Above far left: Photograph published by Beattie of "the mat of the Lost Tribe found at Bligh Sound by Paddy Gilroy in 1842", but the caption was changed later by W. A Taylor. (*H. Beattie*)

Above left: The great overhanging cliff of the "Cave of the Hawea". Note inner dry floor for sleeping and outer cooking area scattered with charcoal fragments. (*J. Hall-Jones*)

Above: Bank of the Wild Natives River where the *Acheron* surveyors came on the Hawea making their escape through the thick undergrowth. (*J. Hall-Jones*)

Left: Closer look at cooking area showing fragments of charcoal and burnt bones. (*J. Hall-Jones*)

stream running off Mt Alarm, a reliable source of water for the Hawea.

Continuing up the fjord with its lofty, craggy peaks, we camped for the night in Gilroy's Amazon Cove. The next day we kayaked to the head of the fjord and paddled up Wild Natives River, where in 1851 the *Acheron* surveyors came across the fugitive Hawea. Captain Stokes records: "About two miles from the mouth of the river the *Acheron*

Mouth of the Wild Natives River where Grave's party arrived out at the head of Bligh Sound in 1900 and also twice again. (*J. Hall-Jones*)

party came on the fresh footmarks of some natives, who were making their escape through the thick underwood. The people as far as we could learn, belong to a small, isolated and almost unknown tribe, rarely seen by their own countrymen, by whom they are called the wild men of the mountains." Appropriately Stokes named the river "Wild Natives River".

What happened to the "flax mat" that was taken from the "Cave of the Hawea" by Paddy Gilroy in 1842? Herries Beattie in his book *The Maoris of Fiordland* (1949) publishes a photograph of an elderly Maori wearing "the mat of the Lost Tribe found at Bligh Sound by Paddy Gilroy in 1842". It should be noted, however, that the "flax mat" looks more like a cloak than a mat, and that the photograph was taken by W. A. Taylor in 1932.

A year later, W. A. Taylor published his own book, *Lore and History of the South Island Maori* (1950), in which he reproduces the same photograph that he took in 1932 and corrects Beattie's caption. The mat (cloak) was found in Dusky Sound, not Bligh Sound, states Taylor. The mat found in Bligh Sound "was one decorated with kiwi feathers".

In the slender hope that the "flax mat" may have been handed into a museum I wrote to both the Otago and Canterbury Museums, but neither were in possession of it. It would appear that the historic mat has gone into limbo.

The Overlanders

In 1900 "Bill" Grave and his companions arrived out at the mouth of Wild Natives River having discovered a route from the North Fiord of Lake Te Anau over Oilskin Pass and down Wild Natives River to the head of Bligh Sound. At the mouth of Wild Natives River "we erected signal poles to mark our successful crossing", recounts Grave. "Our first night at the Sound was rather exciting", he continues. "We had camped near the entrance [of the river] to the Sound [but it had been raining heavily all week] and by nightfall the river had risen above its banks, invading the bush-covered flat all around us, leaving us on a little island scarcely bigger than the tent." It was suggested that they take to the trees, but the prospect of spending the night perched in the branches with

Photograph by Richard Henry of a Fiordland crested penguin on its nest. Note crest and characteristic white stripes on its face. (*Hocken Library*)

"Bill" Grave (standing) and Arthur Talbot, who almost lost his life on the Worsley Pass to Bligh Sound in 1903. (*Alexander Turnbull Library*)

Members of Grave's expedition to Bligh Sound in 1902. From left: Thomas ("Oilskin") Hunter, A. C. ("Crusoe") Gifford and "Bill" Grave. (*Alexander Turnbull Library*)

the rain pelting down was not very inviting and they moved camp to higher ground. But they were still not out of danger and during the night there was a loud crash overhead. "Morning light revealed that a big dead tree had [fallen] right across our tent but had been held up by the branches of other trees – a lucky escape!" the explorers returned over Oilskin Pass, which they named after Thomas Hunter, nicknamed "Oilskin" because of his habit of applying oil to his sensitive skin whenever the sun appeared, which wasn't too often!

Two years later (in 1902) they recrossed their route over Oilskin Pass to Bligh Sound, "this time selecting a camping ground a foot or two higher than the last. As we dried out our clothes, which had now been wet for a week, a penguin stood a couple of yards from the fire, a most interested spectator. We took a photo of him and when we left he was still standing there." (This was presumably a Fiordland crested penguin, of which Deiter and I saw a number in Bounty Haven in 2001.) The party ventured out onto the tidal mudflats of Wild Natives River, but by the time they returned the tide had risen and they almost lost A. C. ('Crusoe') Gifford in a deep pool. They had taken to a tree to avoid the rising water, but when it came to "Crusoe's" turn to climb the tree it snapped and "all we saw of 'Crusoe' was his hat floating quietly on the surface of the deep pool". Happily a moment later the owner reappeared and took repossession of his hat.

The following year (1903) the explorers returned to Bligh Sound, this time finding a new route from the Worsley Arm of Lake Te Anau over Worsley Pass to the Sound. As they climbed back over Worsley Pass, Arthur Talbot slid

The Clio Rock

In 1871 Commodore F. H. Stirling of *HMS Clio* was conducting Governor Sir George Bowen and his wife on a cruise of the West Coast Fjords, when the *Clio* struck an uncharted, submerged rock in Bligh Sound. Accompanying the vice-regal party was Sir James Hector, who had earlier traversed the route from Martins Bay to Queenstown. Hector volunteered to retrace his route to Queenstown and summon help. Heading north by boat to Martins Bay he walked through to Queenstown, where a message was telegraphed to Dunedin. Two days afterwards the *Stormbird* arrived in Bligh Sound and assisted the *Clio* to Milford Sound. It was during the vice-regal visit that the Bowen Falls were named after the Governor's wife, Lady Bowen, and the Stirling Falls after Commodore Stirling.

The hazardous Clio Rock is now marked clearly on the chart, about halfway along the east side of the middle reach of the fjord, but it is still given a wide berth by prudent skippers.

Photograph from the vicinity of Clio Rock looking across at the sharp lines of Turn Round Point, with the entrance reach behind. (*J. Hall-Jones*)

Right: Stina Beach in the main reach, with the bend leading into Bounty Haven behind. (*J. Hall-Jones*)

and disappeared over a precipice. His companions thought he was a "goner", but by the greatest of good fortune he was "caught up by his swag after falling 30 feet." Still out of view, his companions were greatly relieved to hear a plaintive call from below, "Get my hat!" On his being hauled up he denied indignantly that he had been frightened as he dangled in space. "What do you think I did while I was hanging there", he said. "I took out my watch, felt my pulse, and found it was normal!" The same Arthur Talbot later discovered the Grave-Talbot route to Milford Sound with Grave.

CHAPTER 7

Gold Rush at Preservation Inlet

Minerals are the hope of the place, but failing all Preservation Inlet will remain a safe retreat for the distressed mariner, or where the man of science can retire for a while and examine into the mysteries of nature.
A. Johnston, 1868

Originally called Preservation Harbour by the early sealers, Preservation Inlet was known to the Maori as Rakituma, the "threatening sky". A highly appropriate name for this storm-prone fjord in the south-west corner of New Zealand. This southernmost fjord was once the scene of two Maori battles, the first whaling station in New Zealand and a major gold rush in the 1890s.

Right: A "threatening sky" over the entrance of "Rakituma" (Preservation Inlet). (*J. Hall-Jones*)

The Battles at Spit Island

In 1780 the Hawea tribe rose against the Ngaitahu settlers on the Otago Peninsula, killing several, then fleeing round the coast to Spit Island in remote Preservation Inlet. A flat-topped stack, Spit Island is connected by a sandy spit to the mainland at low tide. Encompassed by steep-walled seacliffs with a good lookout towards the sea, it was a perfect, natural fortress for a tribe in fear of pursuit.

Vowing revenge for the massacre, Tarewai, a big Samson-like chief of the Ngaitahu, pursued the Hawea to Spit Island in a war canoe. But as he lay offshore that

The sandspit where Maru acted like a seal and the bay where Tarewai anchored his war canoe. (*J. Hall-Jones*)

Spit Island with its sandspit at low tide. Cavern Head in immediate foreground. In the distance a narrow isthmus leads through to South Port in Chalky Inlet. (*J. Hall-Jones*)

The limestone slab in Cavern Head where the petrified man was found. (*R. Johnson*)

night, a Hawea warrior swam out and attached a flax rope to the bow of the war canoe. The canoe was gently hauled ashore, where according to one tradition all the occupants were slain and the chief's body was consumed. In a different version it is said that Tarewai managed to escape and swim to Cavern Head where, mortally wounded, he crawled inside and died.

This second version could explain the petrified man found at Cavern Head by Walter Traill of the cutter *Rosa* in 1877. "Close to the head of the cave", records Traill, "we discovered the body of a man cemented into the floor by the action of drops percolating through from the limestone roof. It was a large skeleton lying on its back with the lower limbs stretched out and the arms tucked up under the sides."

Traill reported his discovery to Dr Hector who, disregarding Maori sensitivity, told Traill to remove the skeleton. In the interim period the skeleton was quietly uplifted by Maori and interred elsewhere.

In 1898 some miners found a greenstone mere inside the cave. Whereas the blade of the mere was heavily encrusted with limestone, the handle was comparatively free,

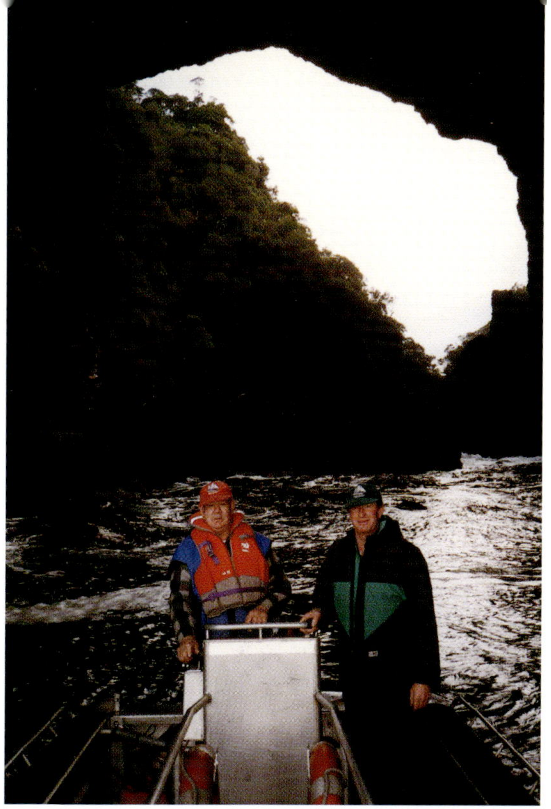

soft bowenite it was an ornamental mere, a symbol of the authority of a great chief such as Tarewai.

Meantime, learning of Tarewai's debacle, another Ngaitahu chief, the great Maru, took off to settle the debt. Approaching Spit Island under cover of darkness he concealed his men among the rocks at the foot of the fortress. Dressing himself up in a sealskin he flopped his way out in the surf to the sandspit, where he arched himself up like a seal. In the morning light the unsuspecting Hawea leaped joyfully

Entering the cavern of Cavern Head. (*J. Hall-Jones*)

Above right: Tarewai's greenstone mere which was encrusted with limestone when found in Cavern Head. Note slender shaft and absence of hole for a wrist thong. (*Courtesy Reva Calvert*)

Right: The tidal sandspit of Spit Island, where Maru acted like a seal while his men lay in ambush among the rocks. (*D. Kraft*)

suggesting that the owner had once been holding it. Believing it to be Tarewai's mere the miners took it to Invercargill businessman John Kingsland who was closely associated with Maori and he purchased it from them. John Kingsland removed the encrustations with a grindstone to reveal a beautiful translucent bowenite (takiwai) mere with a slender shaft and without the usual hole for a wrist thong, as in a fighting mere. Made of

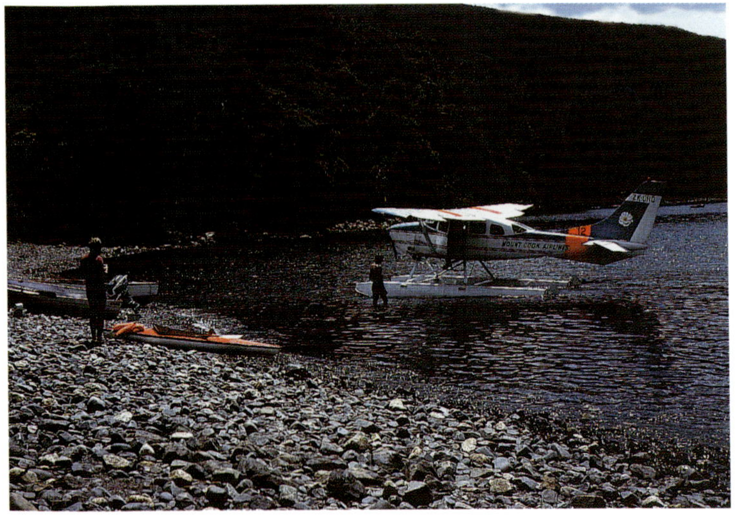

The stony beach at Cuttle Cove whaling station. The boats are at the mouth of the station's freshwater stream. (*J. Hall-Jones*)

down from their fortress to procure this welcome addition to their larder, fell into the ambush and were slaughtered.

But not all the Hawea were killed, for a party had been away hunting at the time. Returning to Spit Island on the fateful morning they saw what had happened and fled up the coast to Bligh Sound. (See previous chapter.)

The Whaling Station at Cuttle Cove

In 1822 Captain West of the whaler *Indian* put into Preservation Inlet. "A whale suddenly spouted in the sound and the captain lowered away and made fast. Lashing out with its tail, the whale smashed the boat to slivers; sending the sailors broadcast on the waters. Rounding on Captain West it picked him up in its huge jaws, severely mauling him. West died a few days later and was buried on an island at the entrance to the sound." Ro Carrick's story of West's fatal encounter suggests that he was attacked by the fiercest of all whales, the sperm or "Moby Dick" whale, known to have sunk ships.

Cuttle Cove has always been recognised as the safest anchorage in Preservation Inlet. With a permanent stream of

Left: Edwin Palmer, who took over from Williams as manager of the whaling station. (*Hocken Library*)

freshwater, an easy beach to land on and a flat foreshore to build on, it was the ideal spot for a whaling station. In 1829 Peter Williams, acting for George Bunn & Co of Sydney, purchased the land from the Maori for the price of 60 muskets. During that same year Williams established the station and by the end of the year it had produced 120 tuns of whale oil.

With a large house for Williams and his family, six houses for the staff of 60 men, a large store for 300 tons of goods and a boatshed for 16 whaleboats, it was a substantial settlement. It is now recognised as the first whaling station to operate in New Zealand. (A smaller station was founded in Marlborough by John Guard in the same year, but it was not producing oil until two years later.)

Williams ran the station for five years, then it was bought out by Johnny Jones and Edwin Palmer, with Palmer acting as manager for the next three years until it closed down in 1836. Statistics show that the station averaged 150 tuns of whale oil annually for its eight years of operation (1829-1836) and that the best year was 1835 when 46 whales were caught, with the production of 176 tuns of whale oil.

As co-owner of the station, Johnny Jones visited

Left: Johnny Jones, co-owner of the whaling station with Palmer. He later founded a chain of stations around the south coast. (*A. Eccles*)

Piece of whalepot found at Cuttle Cove in 1968. (*J. Hall-Jones*)

Mounting the plaque at the site of the first whaling station in New Zealand. (*J. Hall-Jones*)

Cuttle Cove in 1835 and was so impressed with what he saw that he proceeded to set up a whole chain of whaling stations around the south coast to become New Zealand's famous whaling magnate.

Edwin Palmer was still at Cuttle Cove in 1837 when the whaler *Bombay* put into Preservation Inlet. During the night a storm blew up, driving the *Bombay* onto the rocks. The next day, with the sea still "feather white", Palmer risked his life when he set off in a longboat, laid out a stream anchor and the *Bombay* was hauled off the rocks.

It was a hard lonely life at the station and six of the hands set out for the 'day' in a whaleboat, never to return. As at least four of them turned up later on Stewart Island, it is concluded that they had decided to take 'French leave'. In 1837 an 18 year old lad, Charles Denahan, wrecked one of the boats on the rocks and Palmer took a rope to him, as was the punishment in those days. Unfortunately Denahan was suffering from an internal complaint at the time and he died three weeks later. Palmer was tried for manslaughter in Sydney, but was acquitted.

With the killing of both whale calves and their mothers it was a 'robber' industry and by eight years the whaling station had run itself out of business. When the Antarctic explorer John Balleny called at the station in 1838 he reported it as an "old one, deserted".

When the *Acheron* surveyed Cuttle Cove in 1851 it gave the name "Single Tree Island" to the island at the entrance to the cove. Although the island is now completely covered with bush the name suggested that the whalers may have cleared it, leaving a single tree as a lookout for spotting whales coming into the inlet to calf. I was therefore delighted to come across a sketch (in 1897) showing a bare island with only one tree on it.

As the first whaling station in New Zealand, Cuttle Cove seemed worthy of a plaque. In 1968 the author, with the assistance of three friends (Jahn Kionig from the fjords of Norway, Alistair Carey and Brian Reid), mounted a bronze plaque on a large rock on the beach of Cuttle Cove. On the bank of the freshwater stream

Below: Humpback whale leaping out of the sea at the entrance to Milford sound. (*M. Darroch*)

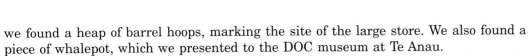

Left: Bishop Selwyn's schooner, the *Undine,* being "tossed about like a cockleshell". *(Selwyn papers)*

Below: Bishop Selwyn at the helm of the *Undine.* (*Selwyn papers*)

we found a heap of barrel hoops, marking the site of the large store. We also found a piece of whalepot, which we presented to the DOC museum at Te Anau.

Today, cruise guides and fishermen are spotting more and more whales on the Fiordland coast, suggesting that the devastated population is making a comeback.

A Sermon in the Wilderness

Early in 1851 *HMS Acheron*, after battling against a severe storm, finally made it into Preservation Inlet, where she remained surveying for the next three weeks. Accompanying her was the schooner *Otago* acting as a tender.

On 31 January Bishop Selwyn arrived in his schooner *Undine* on a marathon tour of his huge diocese. Unhappy about his chronometer he tracked the *Acheron* down to Cuttle Cove for a check.

His Lordship held divine service on board the *Acheron* on Sunday. Archibald Fullerton, who was serving in the *Acheron* at the time, describes the scene:

HMS Acheron which was twice driven back by a storm in Broke-adrift Passage before entering Chalky Inlet. Painted from a sketch by Capt. F. J. Evans. (*National Library of Australia*)

"I've never forgotten the service because it impressed me so much. There we were in this wild outlandish place, on the deck of a ship on which church service was being conducted for us by a bishop in full canonicals. Aye, he was a fine stamp of a man and what a fine voice he had. It was the sort of voice that thrilled one through and through. As we stood there on the quarter-deck he gave us a fine description of the gale which had driven him to shelter in the cove where he had found us at anchor. He said, 'Our frail little craft was tossed about like a cockleshell, as the mountainous seas sought to overwhelm us, but our faith was strong in Him who had dominion over the waters of the earth'."

A few days later the great man departed for the Auckland Islands in the *Undine.*

After completing the survey of Preservation Inlet the *Acheron* attempted to move on to Chalky Inlet, but was driven back twice by storms. She took the *Otago* in tow but the hawsers snapped in "Broke-adrift Passage" and the *Otago* was driven back into "Otago's Retreat". Finally the legendary whaler Tommy Chasland piloted the *Acheron* round Gulches Head (which separates the two inlets) into "the long-sought" Chalky Inlet.

Right: Sketch plan for the Puysegur Point Lighthouse by Charles Heaphy V.C., 1874. Note the "Landing Place" and also the "coal mine" and "wharf". (*Alexander Turnbull Library*)

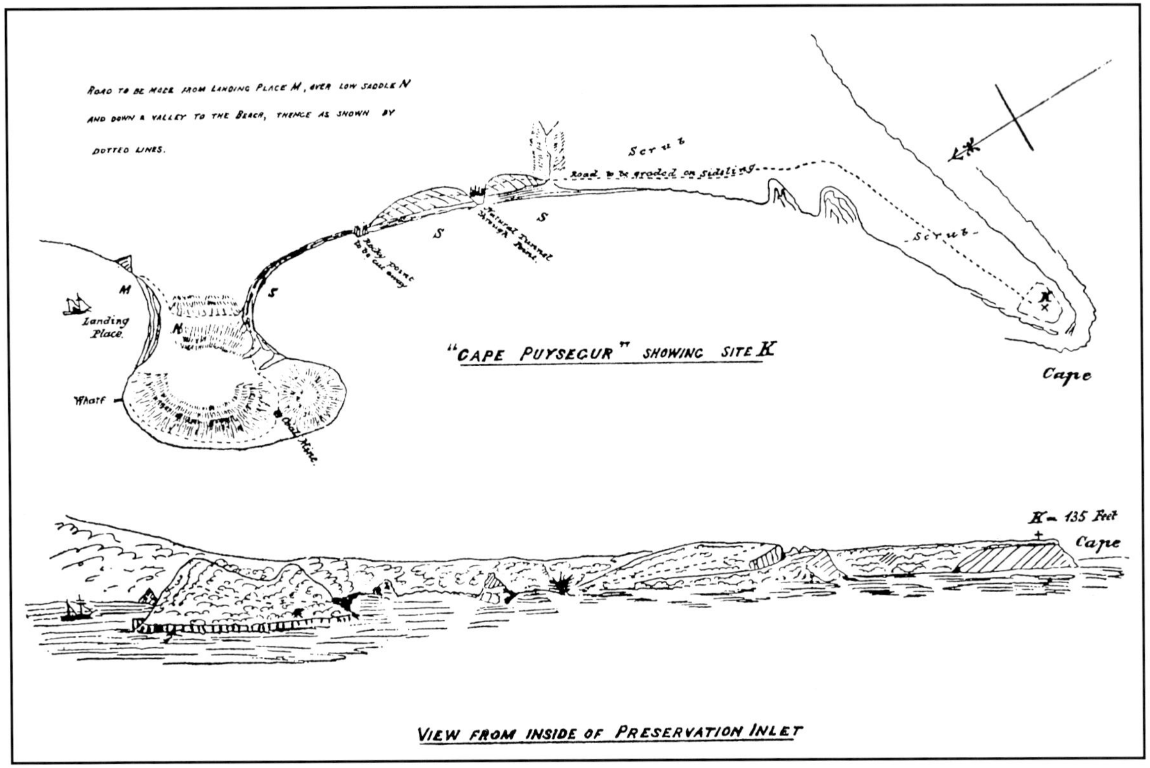

The original lighthouse tower was 60 feet high and was built of wood. It was first lit on 1 March 1879. (*Rakiura Museum*)

Puysegur Point Lighthouse

After *HMS Clio* was nearly wrecked in Bligh Sound with Governor Sir George Bowen aboard, it was the Governor himself who suggested that the coast should be surveyed for a lighthouse. Puysegur Point, jutting out from the entrance of Preservation Inlet, was the obvious place for a light, most of the traffic being concentrated on this south coast.

In 1874 the government steamer *Luna* landed a party of surveyors, including the surveyor-artist Charles Heaphy VC, at the "Landing Place" in Otago's Retreat, as shown on Heaphy's sketch. Setting out from the "Landing Place" they surveyed a road over a "low saddle" and "down a valley to a beach". From there the road would be "graded on sideling" up on to the point and so out to the very tip, which they recommended as an excellent position for a lighthouse. From there the Solander Islands could be seen away to the east and Cape Providence away to the west. "A light from a tower 60 feet high would be visible for 20 miles", they estimated.

Their recommendations were accepted and in 1875 a working party was put ashore at the landing place. The trees and scrub were cleared along the line of the road to the lighthouse and the site prepared for building. By 1879 the whole project was completed, with an oil store at the landing and a dray road up to the 60 foot lighthouse, which was built of Australian hardwood. John Ericson was appointed as the principal keeper and the light was lit for the first time on 1 March 1879.

The Coal Mine

Interestingly, Heaphy's sketch also shows a "coal mine" on a headland near the "Landing Place", with a track leading round to a "wharf".

The first report of coal in Preservation Inlet was by Dr Charles Forbes of the *Acheron*, who discovered it on "Preservation Island", as it was named originally by the sealers. In honour of Dr Forbes' discovery, Captain Stokes took the liberty of changing the sealers' name to Coal Island.

In 1867 J. J. Coates, a mining surveyor, discovered a seam of coal on the headland opposite Coal Island, as shown on Heaphy's map. His party drove a tunnel into the seam on the cliff face. But there wasn't a hope of loading coal into boats on the exposed beach below the mine, so they cut a roadway to a landing stage on a more sheltered side of the headland. But nothing else happened.

The oil store which was built at the "Landing Place". The white picket fence on the left surrounds the cemetery. (*J. Hall-Jones*)

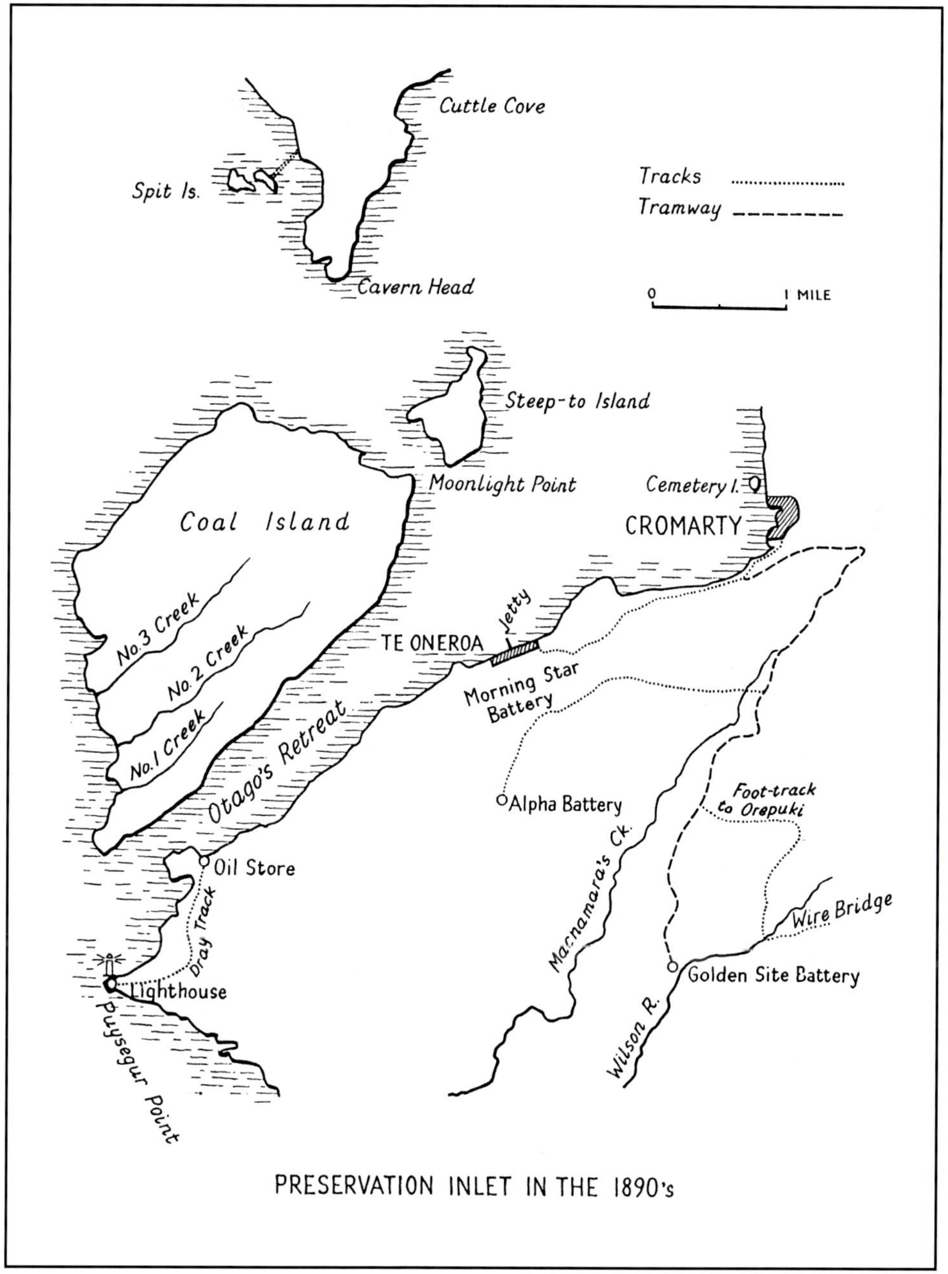

Diagram of the Preservation Inlet goldfield in the 1890s. (*Copyright J. Hall-Jones*)

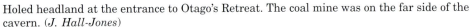

Holed headland at the entrance to Otago's Retreat. The coal mine was on the far side of the cavern. *(J. Hall-Jones)*

Above right: Stone-wall channel constructed by Cullen and Clark at Moonlight Point. *(J. Hall-Jones)*

Right: Moonlight Point, where Louis Longuet picked up a 16 ounce nugget in the shingle. *(D. Kraft)*

Then in 1869 Captain James Greig was commissioned by a coal mining company to report on the mine. The "coal pit" had to be cleaned out, the roof shored up and rails laid for a trolley. The biggest job of all was to clear the slips on the road to the landing stage. A "sort of jetty" was built out with a "sort of crane", so that bags of coal could be slung out into boats for loading on to the schooner. 45 tons of coal were mined and shipped out by Captain Greig and his crew and sold by the company. But this was the only shipment from the mine and after the discovery of better coal in Otago and Southland, the mine was abandoned.

Gold Discovered

In 1885 Philip Payn was appointed as a probationary assistant keeper at the lighthouse. At first he worked well and in a few months he was promoted to assistant keeper. On his days off he rowed across to Coal Island where he began working a claim. His times off tended to become extended and finally in 1887 when he failed to turn up for duty he was sacked. Philip Payn had discovered gold on Coal Island and quite unperturbed he moved over to the island to prospect full time.

The news slowly trickled out and by 1890 there were 70 miners working the four creeks at the seaward end of the island. Naming the creeks simply by numbers, 1 to 4, they concentrated their efforts on No. 2 Creek, where Payn and his mates had put in a water race from a lake in the interior. None of the nuggets were big, the largest being 3 ounces, but by the end of the year a total of 400 ounces of gold had been recovered.

By far the largest nugget found on Coal Island was a 16 ounce nugget which Louis Longuet picked up amid the shingle on Moonlight Point, at the other end of the island. Also at Moonlight Point, Cullen and Clark constructed a spectacular stone-wall channel, which is still there.

Miners panning a creek for gold. (*Alexander Turnbull Library*)

THE GOLD BATTERIES

Golden Site Battery and Cromarty

With the discovery of gold on Coal Island the search soon spread over onto the mainland, into the deep ravines of the Wilson River and Sealers Creek, behind Puysegur Point. Working their way up the Wilson River gorge, prospectors came across nuggets with sharp quartz attached, suggesting that there was a mother lode upriver and not too far away.

It was James Smith who found the reef and then only by accident. In 1892 when he was felling a tree it toppled on another, tearing it out by the roots to expose the quartz reef with nuggets studded all over the surface. The miners "lost their heads in their excitement" and they determined to get a quartz crushing stamper battery in as soon as possible. But herein lay the problem – the reef was 200 metres down at the bottom of a precipitous gorge and several kilometres across a high broken plateau from the sea.

HOTEL

Facing page, far left: Panorama of Cromarty foreshore showing McIntyre's sawmill and wharf at the south end of the beach. (*Rakiura Museum*)

Facing page, left: North end of the beach showing store and post office at the foot of the main wharf (cut off in photo). A corner of the hotel on right and the school at the far end. Docherty Island in distance. (*Rakiura Museum*)

Facing page, far below left: The two-storeyed Kisbee Hotel at Cromarty. (*Otago Settlers Museum*)

Facing page, below left: Golden Site mine in the gorge of the Wilson River. Battery shed on the extreme left with pipeline leading down from water race. Trolley line from the mine-head (the turret-shaped building). (*Rakiura Museum*)

Below: The ten-stamper quartz crushing battery of the Golden Site mine. (*J. Hall-Jones*)

To bring the heavy stamper battery in, an eight kilometre wooden tramline would have to be constructed from Kisbee Bay up onto the plateau and along to the top of the gorge, where the battery would be sledged down to the bottom.

To service the whole project, the town of Cromarty was laid out at Kisbee Bay, with a wharf built out from the foreshore, a store and post office, a two-storeyed hotel (the Kisbee Hotel), two boarding houses and even a school. John McIntyre established a sawmill to cut the timber for the houses and the tramline.

The boiler of John McIntyre's sawmill in 1995. (*J. Hall-Jones*)

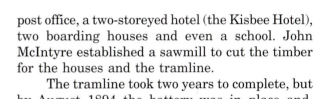

The tramline took two years to complete, but by August 1894 the battery was in place and, driven by a water wheel, it began crushing the quartz for gold. By the end of the year 875 ounces of gold had been recovered. But the following year the returns dropped off steeply to just 111 ounces. The mine had run out of reef and although it carried on intermittently the battery was finally closed down in 1901.

Today the ten-stamper battery still stands proudly on the edge of the Wilson River. The wooden houses of Cromarty have rotted away and been overgrown by bush. But a huge rhododendron (*Cunningham's white*) has survived and flowers incongruously in the native bush. Further along the beach is the boiler of John McIntyre's sawmill. A few years ago the modern Cromarty Lodge was built on the site of the old gold town.

Morning Star Battery and Te Oneroa

Fortunately, as the hopes of the Golden Site mine were fading, the line of the quartz reef was picked up again at Te Oneroa (Long Beach), this time more conveniently beside the inlet. Specimens of gold-bearing quartz had been found frequently at the mouth of the creek at Te Oneroa and in 1894 George Holloway and Donald McKenzie decided to follow the creek up to see if there was a mother lode higher on the hillside. As they ascended the steep gully Holloway slipped, pulling out a tussock to reveal an outcrop of quartz studded with gold.

Winch and aerial cableway to carry the timber props up to the mines. The winchman is standing on a platform at the foot of the wharf. (*Rakiura Museum*)

The township of Te Oneroa at Long Beach in 1898. The Morning Star battery can be seen in the trees directly behind the wharf. (*Burton Bros.*)

The Morning Star Company was formed and a ten-stamper quartz crushing battery was brought in. Because of the lack of water on the hillside the battery was driven by steam and by the first year of operating (1895) it had yielded 728 ounces of gold.

To serve the whole mine the town of Te Oneroa was laid out on the foreshore immediately below

George Holloway, who discovered the Morning Star mine and lived to the age of 100. (*R. Munro*)

the battery, with a store and post officc, a social hall, school, boarding houses and private houses. A long wharf was run out from the shore, from which a winch and aerial cableway conveyed timber props up to the mines on the steep hillside above. From these mines, trolleys, running on a wooden tramline, carried the quartz down to the battery for crushing.

The Morning Star mine did

Closer look at the Morning Star battery, showing the large battery shed on left and the boiler house on right. (*Burton Bros*)

Mine drive near the battery, 1972. The pit props have since collapsed and the mine has filled with ooze. (*L. Morris*)

Right: Collapsed uprights of the Crown Battery in 1979. (*J. Hall-Jones*)

considerably better than the Golden Site mine and carried on for a much longer time. Its highest yield was in 1896 when 3,420 ounces of gold were recovered.

Some of the piles of the long Te Oneroa wharf still survive on the foreshore of the old gold town. But with the easy access from the sea, most of the Morning Star battery was removed during the War for scrap metal. Nevertheless, the camshaft of the battery and the boiler remain, also the concrete foundations of the battery.

Crown Battery

I was unaware that there was a battery at Cuttle Cove until I came across mention of it in the *Annual Reports of the Goldfields*. "The five-stamper Crown Battery came from Waipori", the report informed me, "and was re-erected at Cuttle Cove in 1892. But the first year's crushings did not come up to expectations, and when a tree fell across it, badly damaging the framework, it was abandoned."

Armed with this knowledge, I landed with a DOC party at the mouth of a waterfall, just north of Cuttle Cove. There on the bank beside the waterfall were the collapsed uprights of the battery, one of the five stampers and a mine drive.

Scrambling up beside the waterfall we followed an old tramline along the bank of the stream to discover two more mine drives beside another waterfall.

Alpha Battery

I first learned about the Alpha Battery from ranger Phil Dorizac, who rediscovered it in the rough, bushclad country between the Morning Star and Golden Site mines in the early 1960s. But after Phil died no one was able to find it again.

The Alpha battery (or 'Alphabetery', as Phil referred to it in his racy style) had been hauled in by sledge in 1898, along a branch line of the Golden Site tramline. It was this branch line that had caused all the difficulty in finding the battery as it petered out after 100 metres and had become completely overgrown by a thick tangle of bush.

In 1977 the author with the assistance of an old mining map and two experts with the compass, Lieutenant Bruce Miles SAS and Kevin Mischewski, homed in on the water race system of the battery. Following the pipeline down we found the battery, still standing in all its glory, at the edge of Sealers Creek. Here were the "elephants feet" (the ten stampers) that Phil had talked about and his two "iron brollies" (Berdan crushing bowls).

Being made of iron the Alpha battery proved to be the best preserved of all four batteries on the goldfield. Hidden away from vandals, all the machinery was still lying around and we were able to work out the mechanics of the whole battery. The water pipe that we had followed down would play into the cups of the Pelton water wheel, spinning it to rotate the giant fly wheel of the battery. We were able to turn the fly wheel manually, rotating the camshaft and releasing a stamper rod which crashed down on some quartz lying in the stamper box. After this initial crushing the quartz would be transferred to the Berdan bowls, which would be spun with heavy metal

Above right: The Alpha Battery today. Note giant fly wheel, camshaft and ten stamper rods all out of phase. Ten stamper weights in stamper box. (*J. Hall-Jones*)

Right: The Pelton water wheel for the Alpha Battery. Note large cups. (*J. Hall-Jones*)

Safe with door ajar, as found in 1977. (*J. Hall-Jones*)

The only known picture of the Alpha mine. The large building behind the trees on the left is the battery shed. The tramline is coming from the minehead. Miners' huts on right. (*Rakiura Museum*)

balls inside to produce finer crushing. The final extraction process would be with cyanide. There was even a safe beside the battery, but the door was ajar and there was not a grain of gold inside!

Behind the battery we found the deep mine shaft and a pair of giant winding wheels for bringing the quartz up to the surface. From there the quartz would be carried in trolleys along the tramline (as seen in the old photograph) to the battery for crushing. Near the mine shaft were the remains of the miners' huts, with the usual accumulation of old bottles lying around.

The Alpha Battery's first year of operating (1898) was its best year, yielding 301 ounces of gold. The problem was to obtain enough water on this high plateau to drive the battery. In 1908 the claim was taken over by Louis Longuet (of Moonlight Point fame) for ground sluicing.

Tarawera Smelter

The reclining brick chimney of the Tarawera smelter in Isthmus Sound impresses everyone who sees it. Equally so, the large brick blasting furnace at the base of the chimney.

Why a reclining chimney and why a blasting furnace? The ore at the

The two Berdan spinning bowls for finer crushing. (*J. Hall-Jones*)

The reclining brick chimney of the Tarawera smelter. (*N. Collinson*)

The large brick blasting furnace at the base of the chimney. (*R. Delamore*)

Tarawera mine consisted of a strange mixture of gold, copper, silver and lead. To obtain the gold, both the rock and the metals would have to be melted at a high temperature and to achieve this air would have to be blasted over high quality coke in a solidly built brick furnace.

The designer and master bricklayer had all this in mind when the Tarawera smelter was constructed in 1910. Both the furnace and the chimney faced to the north, the direction of the prevailing wind. With the chimney laid on the hillside, it and the furnace, would draw the maximum draught from this wind. For the same purpose there would also be a flue on the top of the chimney and although no flue has ever been found, the four bolts on the top of the chimney indicate that this was the case. Extra draught would be provided by blowers from the boiler near the furnace.

The ore from the Tarawera mine would be placed in a crucible mounted on top of the water-jacketed blast furnace and as the rock melted, the heavy metals would sink to the bottom. The useless molten rock would be decanted off the top and run down a chute into the sea, leaving the valuable metal slag at the bottom for further refining.

So much for the theory. Although an assay of the Tarawera ore showed only seven pennyweights of gold (7/20ths of an ounce) present in a ton of rock, which was not very encouraging, it was decided to proceed with the construction of the smelter.

Thanks to William Todd of Invercargill, who backed the venture, we have a valuable collection of photographs showing the construction of the smelter in 1910. Firstly, a cantilever wharf was built out from the steep headland so that the bricks and timber for the construction could be landed. The photographs show the *ss Invercargill* landing the bricks for the chimney and the furnace on the wharf and the wooden framework of the two-storeyed smelter room erected on the terrace above the wharf. The plant for the smelter, the water-jacketed blast furnace, crucible and blowers were all imported from Sydney.

By April 1911 the smelter was completed and open for business. A trial run of 35 tons of ore was smelted and a quantity of metal-containing slag produced. This was sent to Sydney for an estimate of the cost for the final separation of the metals. But this proved to be too expensive and sadly the decision had to be taken to close down the smelter.

Notwithstanding, the Tarawera reclining chimney survives as one of the most extraordinary sights in Fiordland. It is also a monument to the master bricklayer who constructed it.

Tarawera smelter under construction in 1910, with *ss Invercargill* moored alongside the cantilever wharf. (*W. Todd*)

Left: Cast of metal slag from the crucible, showing its internal shape. (*J. Hall-Jones*)

Photograph showing the framework of the two-storeyed smelter room, cantilever wharf and worker's hut on the hillside above. (*W. Todd*)

Left: ss Invercargill landing the bricks for the chimney and furnace on the wharf. (*W. Todd*)

Jules Berg

One of the characters of the goldfield was the little Swedish miner Jules Berg, who arrived at the inlet in 1925. Jules first lived in a little hut at Diggers Creek on the lighthouse road, where he worked as roadman. Then he moved to a bay at Te Oneroa, where he built his ramshackle house with 'bits and pieces' added on in an 'anyhow' fashion.

A little man with a big heart, Jules Berg (correctly Bjork, but he was always known as Jules Berg) was to become a popular favourite among the fishermen and anyone who called at his house. The stories of the giant parsnips that he grew in a manure of rotten fish are legendary, as was the end product,

Jules Berg in his dinghy off his boatshed and house at Te Oneroa. (*W. McIntosh*)

Left: Jules (with pistol) entertaining visitors outside his house. (*W. McIntosh*)

a potent "parsnippy wine" (as he called it) that flowed freely whenever his visitors arrived. As the session progressed Jules would dress up in a costume, his favourite being a cowboy outfit with two large six-shooters slung rakishly from the hip. His hat, a sombrero, had a mixture of rancid butter and kerosene smeared thickly round the brim to keep the sandflies away. He also had a policeman's outfit for keeping order!

His house with its sloping floor was so easy to wash out. The swish of a well-aimed bucket of water did the trick! The walls were even papered, with old photographs from the *Illustrated Weekly News*. It was always an open home to all, but you had to be careful on approaching it at

Far left: Jules dressed up in his cowboy outfit, six-shooters and all. (*M. Hansen*)

Left: Jules dressed as an armed policeman. (*W. McIntosh*)

Below: Jules Berg's house as seen in 1968. (*J. Hall-Jones*)

night because there were booby traps set in the garden for shooting deer.

Every year Jules religiously renewed his miner's licence and when he was not wine-making or entertaining visitors, he worked a small claim in a gully behind the house.

By 1952 his fishermen friends were becoming concerned about Jules, then 72, living in isolation in the wilderness. Kind hands brought him out to Riverton and looked after him till he died later that year. Unfortunately the unique and historic house of the little Swedish miner was later demolished.

Lighthouse Burned Down

Thanks to ex-lighthouse keeper Tom Smith's book *Man the Light (1996)* we at last have the true story of how it all happened. Tom Smith was there at the time!

Lance Thomas was an escapee from the Sunnyside Mental Institution who had fled to Preservation Inlet, where he lived in a hut on Coal Island. A loner, he had a persecution complex that radio waves and the light from the lighthouse were being 'beamed' on him on the island.

Choosing a day when he thought that everyone was away from the lighthouse, he rowed across from the island in broad daylight (not in the dark as previously reported) and set off up the road determined to do away with his tormenters.

It so happened, Tom Smith was on duty that fateful day, 8 February 1942, and on hearing crashing sounds coming from the radio hut he went to investigate. He opened the door to find Thomas smashing the radio equipment. "There was no attempt to threaten me or the other keepers", records Smith, correcting newspaper reports to the contrary. Thomas just took off down the

road and crossed back to his island home.

Tom Smith then noticed that there was smoke issuing from the lighthouse ventilators. "I opened the door and was immediately forced backwards by the heat. I could see that the fire had such a strong hold that there was no chance of saving the old [wooden] building." He then noticed that smoke was coming from a lighthouse keeper's house. But this fire was still confined to a burning couch and he was able to extinguish it.

Meantime, the radio operator was able to repair the damaged radio and get a message out to the Invercargill Police. The next morning the *Toiler* arrived with six policemen aboard, some of them armed. Knowing that Thomas had a rifle, Sergeant Coutts wisely dispersed his men for the day, some of them even went fishing! Then under cover of darkness another keeper, Tim Smith (who had a hut on the island), rowed the policemen across to the island and guided them up the steep track to Thomas' hut. Surrounding the hut the policemen rushed it before dawn, overpowering Thomas who was still in bed. The mentally ill Thomas was taken away in the *Toiler*.

There were two amusing asides to the arsonist's attack on the

Left: A fine photograph of Puyseur Point by Ray Bolderson. The lighthouse on the tip of the point and the storehouse further back. *(Courtesy R. Bolderson)*

Puysegur Point Lighthouse and the keepers' cottages in 1968. (*J. Hall-Jones*)

Above left: Puysegur Point with a wild sea running at the entrance of Otago's Retreat. Coal Island in left background. (*J. Hall-Jones*)

Left: Captain "Bert" Mercer's photograph of the lighthouse on fire on 8 February 1942. (*J. C. Mercer*)

lighthouse. The legendary "Bert" Mercer happened to fly over the burning lighthouse on one of his routine wartime patrols of the West Coast. Seeing the tower on fire he dropped a message, "*Sorry could not blow it out, Capt. Mercer*". Also, a fishing boat coming out of Chalky Inlet was amazed to see no lighthouse on the point. Having heard a plane fly over, the fishermen put two and two together and were convinced that the lighthouse had been bombed. Approaching the landing nervously they were greatly relieved to find a strong contingent of New Zealand Police in control.

The second lighthouse is much lower than the original one. Cape Providence can be seen on the far horizon. (*J. Hall-Jones*)

Completely razed to the ground it was decided to replace the lighthouse with one powered by electricity. The new tower was much lower than the original one and was lit by electric light for the first time on 26 August 1942. As a bonus, the lighthouse keepers now had electricity in their houses. Sadly the lighthouse is now unmanned, run by solar panels and the houses are demolished.

The Lighthouse Farm

In an interesting account of the various animals kept at the lighthouse, Tom Smith tells us that they had two draught horses for sledging the supplies up the road from the landing. There was a stable for the horses in the little clearing, just before the water tank on the final approach to the lighthouse. There was also a fowlhouse beside the stable, but one of the hens preferred laying her eggs in the horses' manger, so that her eggs were tinged with green from the horses' slobber! There were also cows, but no cow bail, so the cows were milked in the horses' stable! Twelve ewes in lamb were also put ashore and Tom drove them up the road to the lighthouse paddock.

Life was happy at the lighthouse, Tom reflects, everyone got on well with each other and the children kept in touch with the outside world by Correspondence School.

The Cemetery

Beside the old oil store at the landing there is a little cemetery surrounded by a picket fence with some graves that have sad stories to tell. Three of them, James Cromarty, P. G. Cameron and M. Sutherland were miners working on

Left: Grave of one of the three miners drowned on crossing from Coal Island on 26 April 1895. (*J. Hall-Jones*)

Below: Taking bearings on the route of the telephone line, 1977. (*J. Hall-Jones*)

Coal Island who were drowned while crossing from the island to pick up mail. Their boat struck the reef as they approached the landing, capsizing, and all three men were drowned. Philip Payn, the discoverer of the gold in Preservation Inlet, was also in the boat, but managed to cling on and was saved.

Two burials in the same enclosure – Mrs Louden and W. Smith – always puzzle visitors. Mrs Louden was the wife of a miner on Coal Island. She became ill and "Bill" Smith, a linesman, rowed across to bring her out. Returning in the dark they struck the reef, capsizing, and both were drowned. The infant's grave, Richard Harte, was the stillborn son of lighthouse keeper Harte and his wife.

From Puysegur Point, looking along the broken, bushclad south coast where the telephone line was laid. (*J. Hall-Jones*)

Telephone Line

In 1896 telephone engineer J. Orchiston and his men spent three weeks in the densely forested and gorged country of the south coast surveying a route for a telephone line to the outside world, 100 kilometres away. Raging rivers were crossed by rafts made of flax stalks and they lived off the land by shooting kakapos, kiwis and wekas. At least one fearless weka fought back when it stole the bolt of Orchiston's rifle, which he had been cleaning; after that they were without firepower.

It took 12 years before the Government decided to proceed with the telephone line, but in 1908 it was laid in the remarkable time of seven months. No orthodox telephone poles were erected. Trees were felled leaving stumps three metres high into which insulator cups were screwed. The telephone line was completed and open for business on 20 July 1908. Maintenance huts were positioned along the track with linesmen ("Bill" Smith was one) to keep the line open. (In 1977 when Bruce, Kevin and I tramped round the coast on our search for the Alpha Battery we found the remains of one of these maintenance huts on Kakapo Hill. Also insulator cups along the line of the telephone wire.)

In a dense forest noted for its heavy windfalls the telephone was out of action more often than in, and in 1925 communication with the outside world was changed from telephone to radio.

Left: HMS Takapu surveying in Long Sound, 1994. *(J. Hall-Jones)*

Left: Sandstone "road to nowhere", Sealers Creek. *(D. Kraft)*

Above right: Cascade Basin waterfall in 'full roar' at the head of Long Sound. *(J. Hall-Jones)*

Right: Sandstone pyramid at the mouth of Sealers Creek. *(J. Hall-Jones)*

Preservation Revisited

In 2000 Dieter and I flew into to Preservation Inlet to spend two weeks kayaking around the multiple bays and islands of this vast sprawling fjord.

Landing for side-tramps on the way we visited some favourite spots in Preservation Inlet: the walk out to the lighthouse where we saw the steep stacks of the Solander Islands rising abruptly from the sea; the mouth of Sealers Creek, where the harsh weather has sculptured the weirdest formations in the soft sandstone; the Alpha Battery which still stands tall in the deep forest; the extraordinary reclining chimney of the Tarawera smelter in Isthmus Sound; and Spit Island Beach where the beautiful tombola sandspit leads out to historic Spit Island.

At the end of the fortnight we paddled to the head of the well-named Long Sound, almost a fjord of its own, where we saw the magnificent Cascade Basin waterfall in 'full roar' after a heavy rainfall.

CHAPTER 8

The White Cliffs of Chalky Inlet

A white clift is on one of the Islands which lies about the middle of the Mouth of the Bay. carved by a glacier.
James Cook, 1773

Commander Richards in his sailing directions for entering Chalky Inlet in 1851, describes the entrance as "well denoted from the seaward by the white cliffs of Chalky Island lying in the centre of it".

These strikingly white cliffs which encompass Chalky Island are one of the spectacular features of the Fiordland coast and several early voyagers remark on them in their journals.

The Maori name for Chalky Inlet, Taiari, a shell necklace, really refers to the white cliffs that surround the island at its entrance. In the same vein, the European name for the fjord, Chalky Inlet, is also derived from the chalky cliffs of Chalky Island.

Captain Cook spotted the "white clift", on an island, "about the middle of the Mouth of the Bay" when he made landfall on the Fiordland coast in the *Resolution* in 1773. Realising that in the mist he had mistaken the entrance of Chalky Inlet for Dusky Sound, he stood

Right: The spectacular white cliffs of Chalky Island at the entrance to Chalky Inlet. (*J. Hall-Jones*)

appearance of the West Cape and Chalky Island New Zealand
Bearing NW dist. 10 or 12 miles -

Captain Kent's sketch of the white cliffs of Chalky Island, 1823. Cape Providence with the Providence Pillar immediately behind, and the long headland of West Cape on the horizon. (*Admiralty*)

Chalky Island from Cape Providence (Boultbee's "Cave Point") with the Providence Pillar on the left and the "dangerous rocks" of the Providence Reef in the foreground. (*J. Hall-Jones*)

off and carried on to his original objective, "Dusky Bay", which is just as well as the *Resolution* would surely have come to grief on the treacherous submerged reefs and rocks on either side of Chalky Island.

Robert Murry records how in 1792 he took two separate bearings on the "remarkable white cliff" at the entrance to Chalky Inlet, as the *Brittania* approached Dusky Sound to drop off its sealing gang in Luncheon Cove.

In 1823 Captain John Kent, in a quest for a cargo of flax for rope-making, entered Chalky Inlet in the cutter *Mermaid*. Kent "sent the boats away to examine the inlets about the sound for flax". When his men returned empty-handed he weighed anchor and sailed out via the Eastern Passage of Chalky Island. In doing so he observed "many dangerous reefs and rocks", two of which would be the notorious Balleny Reef and Table Rock.

Captain Kent drew a little sketch of Chalky Island, showing its prominent white cliffs. Immediately behind the left-hand end of Chalky Island is Cape Providence, with the Providence Pillar off its tip. Beyond Cape Providence is the headland of West Cape.

John Boultbee in 1826 recorded in his journal that:

"About 20 miles S. of Dusky Bay is a large harbour called 'Chalky' from the whiteness of its cliffs. As you go round Cave Point [Cave Providence, which has a tunnel through its tip] you pass several dangerous rocks [the Providence Reef], and here the tide is strong which adds to the danger. Some years ago a boat and crew were lost on one of them.

At Chalky Island is a safe boat harbour [Sealers Bay], where boats may anchor, a reef extending a considerable distance across the entrance, so as to break the seas and render the harbour smooth.

The ship harbour [North Port, the best anchorage in Chalky Inlet] between [Chalky] island and the Main[land] is safe. It branches off in different directions, forming separate bays [of which Fisherman Bay is the main one].

On the East side is a small fresh water river [Kohe Creek at the entrance of South Port]. At the head of the harbour [South Port] are large caves which are dry and form a convenient shelter for boats and crews.

At 5 miles distant from Chalky Island is Table Rock and a number of inferior ones, some scarcely perceptible [Balleny Reef, named after Captain John Balleny]."

A Fatal Accident

"During one of our excursions at this place we met with a shocking accident. We had been to a rock to shoot seal & the boatsteerer & another man had landed for that purpose, one of them fired his musket but without success, & they both returned to the boat, & laid their muskets under the stern sheets of the boat with their muzzles pointing forwards. We pulled off a little distance & then proceeded to lay in our oars, & get the mast up, ready to sail across the Bay. I was pulling a larboard oar, & my body was in a line with the loaded piece as I sat pulling, the man who was abaft, pulling on the starboard side. In the act of leaning over to lay in my oar my body was out of the direction of the musket, as his was *in* the direction, when (whether through the shaking of the boat or not, I cannot say) the piece went off, & lodged the balls in the unfortunate man's head. He fell dead instantly, & did not so much as struggle or move a lineament of his face, indeed he passed from life to death without any visible pain.

Astonished & mute as we were for the moment we were unable to express ourselves; the boatsteerer first breaking the silence by the most extravagant gestures & disconnected language, blaming himself for the poor fellow's death.

One of our people felt the wadding pass his cap & I myself fancied it grazed my hair. The deceased was one of our party when we were attacked by the natives at Open Bay. We

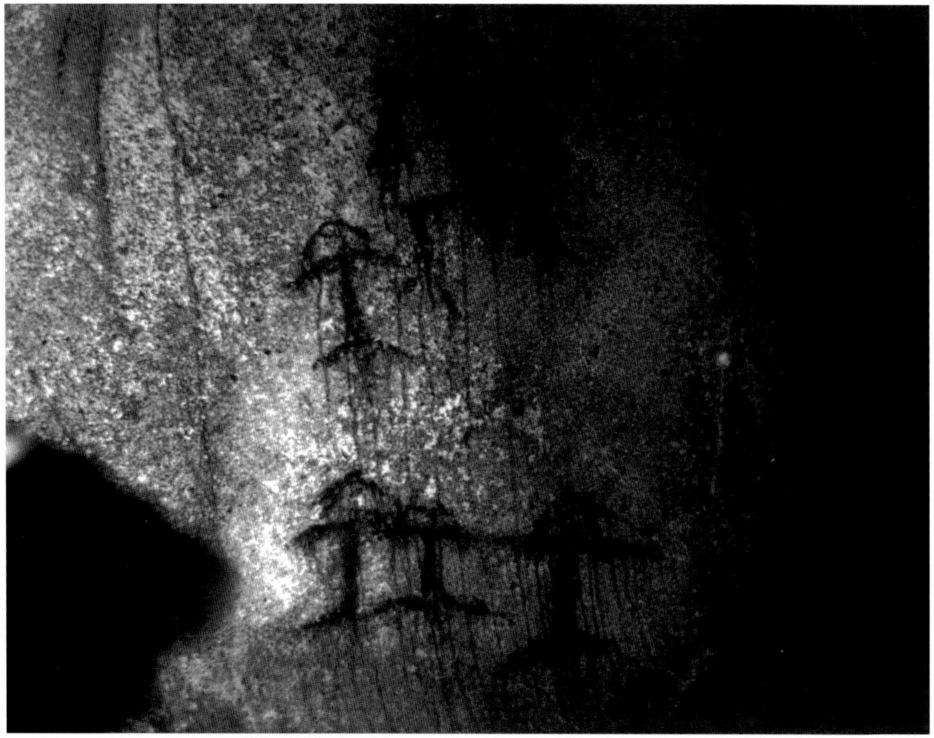

Maori rock drawings found in a cave on Chalky Island by ranger Allan Cragg in 1973. (*A. Cragg*)

now consisted of 3 out of the six who formed the boat's crew in that affray; & this being the second narrow escape I had had since I was on the coast of New Zealand, I naturally seriously reflected on the timely interposition of Providence which thus preserved me."

After the horrific accident the sealers returned to the cave where they had been living to rest and recover from the shock. While they were building a fire, John Boultbee almost met with a fatal accident himself.

"A New Zealander [Maori] & myself had been to the top of the cliff which is over the cave & had been heaving down large logs of wood for the fire. I came down first with a dog; the man remained heaving down more logs & I had just got near the cave almost directly underneath the cliff, when a log fell on the poor animal & killed him. I was barely 2 feet clear of the same piece of wood, which would certainly have killed me had it fallen on me."

The cave where the sealers had been living while sealing in Chalky Inlet was probably at Sealers Bay, Boultbee's "safe boat harbour" on Chalky Island. In 1994 Michael ("Hooky") Walker of *HMNZS Takapu* and I landed on the sandy beach of Sealers Bay and discovered a large cave with the remains of a midden inside. The floor of the cave was flat, dry and looked particularly suitable for living in. There was even native spinach for green vegetables growing outside! Above the cave was a cliff top with trees suitable for firewood. Although neither "Hooky" nor I had a torch with us to examine the interior of the cave, talking to ranger Allan Cragg later, this proved to be the same cave where, in 1973, he found Maori rock drawings on the wall. Like us, Allan didn't have a torch with him at the time, but he was able to photograph the drawings by reflecting sunlight off some tin foil and directing it inside.

'Edwardson's' Chart

In 1822 (one year prior to Captain Kent's visit) Captain William Edwardson, in his sloop *Snapper*, carried out an extensive search for flax along the whole shoreline of Chalky Inlet, including North Port, South Port and the two arms of the inlet, but without success. While doing so he took many soundings along the way, including multiple soundings in North Port, the safest anchorage in the inlet. Edwardson was a talented and proven cartographer and doubtless he had the intention of drawing a map of Chalky Inlet himself. However, on his return to Sydney he learned that the French explorer D'Urville was about to sail for the Fiordland coast, so he generously passed on his detailed findings to D'Urville's cartographer, Jules de Blosseville, instead.

As it turned out, D'Urville never made it to the Fiordland coast. Nevertheless, Blosseville proceeded to produce the first chart of Chalky Inlet (1824) relying almost entirely on Edwardson's findings. As such, the chart can truly be regarded as Edwardson's. In publishing the chart, Blosseville does pay tribute to Edwardson's work by naming the Edwardson Arm after him. He added two French personal names, Canaris (later misspelt Cunaris by Stokes) and Puysegur Point (named after a famous French admiral). Another interesting name on the chart is Preservation Island, the original name for Coal Island before Stokes changed it. Of particular interest are three little "Huttes" at the head of "Port Chalky" (South Port).

The Sealers "Huttes"

Captain Edwardson had hardly dropped anchor at the head of South Port before a sealing gang from the *General Gates* (Captain Abimeleck Riggs) scrambled aboard. The sealers had been left there 17 months previously by their American captain, with only two barrels of salt bacon for food and were in a deplorable state of nutrition. The infamous Captain Riggs was notorious for starving his men and flogging them at the slightest provocation. Thanks to

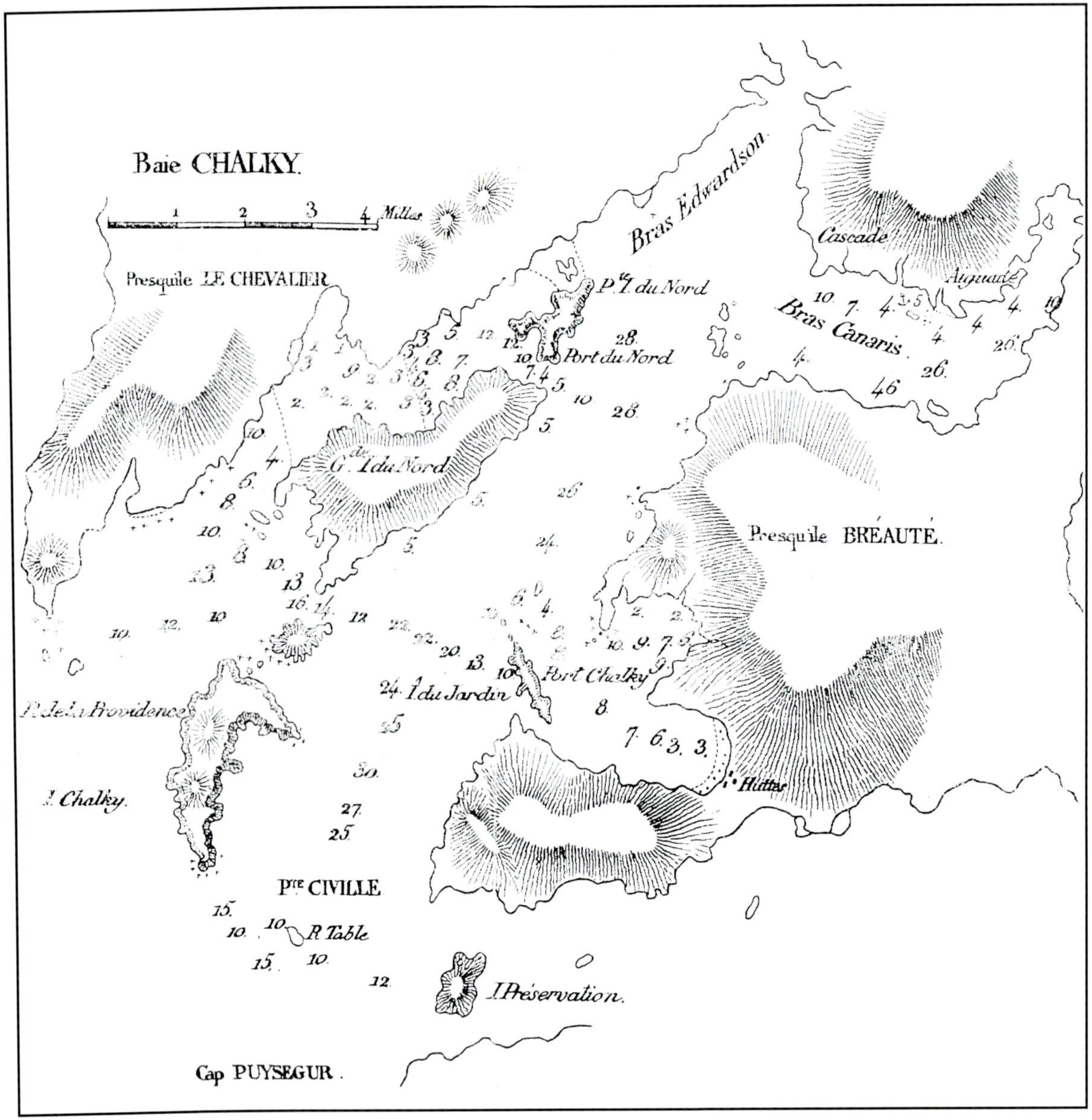

Edwardson's chart of Chalky Inlet as drawn by Jules de Blosseville in 1824. Note French names, Cape Puysegur and Canaris Arm (now misspelt Cunaris Sound) and the three "Huttes" at the head of Port Chalky (South Port). Original name of Preservation Island (now Coal Island) at the entrance to Preservation Inlet. *(R. McNab)*

Left: The beach at the head of South Port, site of the "huttes" of the *General Gates* sealing gang in 1822. *(J. Hall-Jones)*

Left: Boiler of McCallum's sawmill, which was established on the site of the three "huttes" in 1903. *(J. Hall-Jones)*

his same attitude to the Maori a state of warfare existed wherever he left a sealing gang.

After Captain Edwardson had nurtured the human skeletons back to health, the American sealers set off to retrieve a cache of sealskins they had left at General Gates Boat Harbour (on the south coast, beyond Puysegur Point). No sooner had they arrived there than they were attacked by a large party of Maori and were forced to flee back to the *Snapper,* which was still waiting for them in South Port.

Soon after the sealers returned on board their pursuers arrived at the head of the bay, having crossed the isthmus from Spit Island Beach. To Captain Edwardson's astonishment the Maori warriors were led by a tattooed white chief. This turned out to be the famous

James Caddell, who as a lad had miraculously survived a small massacre on Stewart Island and had grown up to become a tattooed chief among his former captors. Thankfully Captain Edwardson was able to strike up a rapport with James Caddell and peace was restored between the two warring parties. Edwardson offered to give Caddell's war party a lift along the south coast in the *Snapper* and even some of the sealers elected to sail as fellow passengers with their former deadly enemies.

Today there is no sign of the three "huttes" of the *General Grant's* sealing gang at the head of South Port. All that can be seen there are the remains of McCallum's sawmill, which was established on the site of the "huttes" in 1903.

Dark Cloud Inlet

Although Tommy Chasland had successfully piloted the *Acheron* into the "long-sought" Chalky Inlet, for most of her time there she lay under a heavy "dark cloud". A darkness which prompted the surveyors alternative name of "Dark Cloud Inlet" for Chalky Inlet. This double-name remained on the chart for over a century until the *Acheron's* name was transferred to the Dark Cloud Range at the head of the inlet.

Landing Bay, where the *Acheron* sheltered behind Cape Providence and the Providence Pillar (seen off the Cape). (*J. Hall-Jones*)

New Zealand Navy resurveying Stokes' Lake Cove at the head of Edwardson Sound, 1994. (*J. Hall-Jones*)

The same "dark cloud" plunged George Hansard into the depths of despair and he wrote:

"Chalky Inlet has the usual dreary landscape, being piled with timber from shore to mountain summit, with no beach visible from our anchorage beyond a few yards of shingle & about the same space of sand at low water.

Blowing a norwester – Strange aspect of the sky, which appears as during an eclipse. Yet the almanack convinces us there is none – Sun totally obscured by a luminous fog filling the atmosphere, except where interrupted by dark cloud directly over the ship – At $^1/_2$ past 11 a.m. the morning resembles a deep twilight, yet the outline of mountain and forest stands out from the sky in boldest relief – Air warm – winds in furious gusts – blowing about the spray in clouds, like dust before a summer's shower. Between decks, lights were necessary as at night – This strange visitation lasted until about 4 o'clock, when a furious rain began, & continued with scarcely any intermission, until Sunday morng."

Gulches Head, in Broke-adrift Passage between Preservation and Chalky Inlets, is widely exposed to all the storms of the Southern Ocean. The dangerous Balleny Reef lies just off to the left. (*J. Hall-Jones*)

Eventually the sun burst through, cheering the scribe's heart:

> "The glorious sun – invisible for so many days, burst out this morning, gladdening every heart, & drying up the deck & our jackets – The notes of birds, all so mute during the late bad weather, peal forth from every bush— cheerfully interrupting the monotonous dullness of this place – where it may be truly said —'Silence sits brooding'."

But it was only a temporary reprieve and they soon plunged back under the "dark cloud".

At least there was plenty of fresh food to be got in this remote, uninhabited corner of Fiordland. "The men caught a great many fish, and crawfish also, with which the western harbours swarm." Dr David Lyall (the ship's surgeon) brought back kiwis and kakapos which had been caught by Sailor.

By 14 February the *Acheron* was ready to depart for Dusky Sound, but the *Otago* still hadn't turned up (she was holed up in Otago's Retreat). So leaving a message for the *Otago* on a white-washed stone at the entrance, the *Acheron* headed out to sea round Cape Providence. But she was soon "baffled". The "wind blew so hard right ahead that she was driven back inside" the entrance. The next morning they "weighed anchor at daybreak and set off on another trial, succeeding this time and puffed into Cascade Cove" later that day.

Hector Dislocates Shoulder

In 1863 Dr Hector's yacht, the *Matilda Hayes*, had the same difficulty as the *Acheron* getting round Gulches Head into Chalky Inlet. With a heavy sea and tide running against it in Broke-adrift Passage the yacht was caught between the great rollers of the Southern Ocean breaking on Gulches Head and the surf boiling on the rocks of Balleny Reef, one of the nastiest places to be caught on the whole Fiordland coast. In spite of a boat out ahead towing, they "began to drift rapidly toward Balleny Reef, which was breaking with great violence about a mile to leeward". So they dropped a kedge in 30 fathoms of water and stood to.

The yacht *Matilda Hayes* which rolled while rounding Gulches Head, dislocating Dr Hector's shoulder. (*J. Buchanan*)

HMNZS Takapu and *Tarapunga* moored in North Port while resurveying Chalky Inlet in 1994. (*J. Hall-Jones*)

"We dreaded having to pass a night in this dangerous position", Hector recounts, "but by good fortune a light breeze sprang up from the SE just before dark, and we lost no time taking advantage of it".

"The yacht rolled heavily and in making sail the main boom broke loose and knocked two of us down, and unfortunately dislocated my shoulder joint. However, with the aid of one of the seamen, I managed to reduce it and have the necessary bandages applied." With the boat out towing in front they got into North Port two hours after dark.

The next day a party set out in the boat to search for some Maoris they had previously encountered in Preservation Inlet. They found them encamped at Landing Bay, inside Cape Providence. "They had killed four seals and had captured a live kakapo", which they sent as a gift to Hector, who was convalescing on the yacht.

"It is rather larger than the common kaka from which, however, it greatly differs in every respect, especially in the form of its bill, which is short and thick. It is of a light green color, with dusky markings; and from having slight whiskers like those of a cat and a depressed circlet of feathers round the eyes, it somewhat resembles an owl. It seemed very uncomfortable when exposed to daylight, but after dusk it became quite lively, climbing about everywhere, displaying all the forward manners of other parrots. He was very ill-tempered and obstinate when interfered with in any of his foraging expeditions, screaming most discordantly and biting furiously. He was rapidly becoming tame, but a fortnight later he was killed by a woodhen, which was foolishly shut up with him in the locker of the boat where he was domiciled."

"North Port is by far the best harbour we have been in up to this time", records Hector. "It is quite land-locked, but opens up so immediately from the wide part of the Inlet, that a large vessel could make right into it without difficulty." (*HMNZS Takapu* and *Tarapunga* used North Port as their base while resurveying Chalky Inlet in 1994.)

The Bird Collector

On 12 January 1887 the *ss Stella* landed Andreas Reischek, the Austrian taxidermist and his assistant, Rimmer, at Fisherman Bay in North Port. After clearing "half an acre of bush", planting a vegetable garden and building a hut at Fisherman Bay, they began to cut two tracks into the depths of the forest. One track followed the river at Fisherman Bay northwards to Lake Rimmer and The Brothers peaks. The other struck southwards to Lake Hector and Landing Bay at Cape Providence. Both lakes were named by Reischek after people who had assisted him in his work. Another lake he named Lake Caesar after his dog, "who actually discovered it when out hunting".

One day while Reischek was travelling along The Brothers track, Caesar took off on the scent of a bird. He was away for a long time and Reischek scolded him on his return. "He looked into my face as much as to say, 'You don't know what I wish to tell you, or you would not scold me'." Reischek followed Caesar along the track, until he suddenly stopped, his nose pointing to the ground. "Upon looking I saw a fine kakapo, which he had got in the morning and carried over two miles, but being a heavy bird he had left it on the track." Continuing on to The Brothers Reischek climbed the highest peak, where he watched one of the finest sunsets he had ever seen:

Amphibian landing in Fisherman Bay, North Port, where Andreas Reischek built his hut in 1887. (*J. Hall-Jones*)

"The sunset which I enjoyed from the highest peak of the Three Brothers was of such magnificent colouring that I had never seen anything to equal it. It would be difficult to paint it with the brush, and is still more difficult to describe in words. Far away the dark blue sea was crested with white foam. The sky, which had been covered up to now

Caesar with the kakapo that he caught on The Brothers track. *(A. Reischek)*

with fleecy clouds, began to lighten with the reflection of the setting sun, glowing with all the colours of the rainbow. From blood-red to orange and gold, the light faded away by gradations to a tender apple-green tinge, out of which the silver moon emerged like a pale Medusa."

On Reischek's southern track towards Landing Bay he "came across a beautiful lake which is not marked on the map. A remarkable thing is that I found not the least sign of life, either fish or insect in it. It lies in from the sea at Breakers Point." (Reischek's description of secluded Lake Hector, as he called it, is perfect. In 1972 our party was struck with the deep silence of Lake Hector. Here nature was totally hushed. But the spell was broken as we headed back towards the inlet and could hear the rollers pounding on Breakers Point.)

During his five months at Fisherman Bay, Reischek collected 37 different species of native birds including kakapo, kokako, native thrush, saddleback and kiwi. But he had a rule of never shooting birds near the hut. "In this way the birds became trustful and observations were much easier." He was able to observe the habits of a pair of "delightful white-throat" (South Island robin) which adopted him at his hut at Fisherman Bay. "They jealously and obstinately guard their own piece of territory against all comers", he records.

"I fed one pair daily and after a few days they readily came into the hut and took food from my hand. They were both so tame that they used to accompany me on my little walks, and while I was digging kiwi or kakapo out of their holes, they would sit by me and pick out the larvae from the loosened earth. Later on they brought their young with them, feeding them with food I gave them. In the early dawn the old birds would enter the hut, perching on the posts of my bunk and the male bird would begin to sing. If I didn't wake at once, they hopped down on my head and began tugging at my hair or beard. When breakfast was ready they used to come and eat off my plate. I could catch hold of them and they showed no sign of fear. When we struck camp it went to my heart to see them sitting lonely and miserable on the bare table."

"The rats are the great enemies of the birds", records Reischek. "Any bird living or breeding near the ground has but a small chance of existing. They play havoc alike with eggs and young and even attack the parent birds."

"I regularly poisoned as many as I could. At night they kept me awake with their noise, knocking things down from the walls, gnawing at my stores and digging holes round the hut. They dug up the potatoes in the garden and dragged them away. On one occasion I hung up poisoned bird-skins, but sure enough the rats climbed on the beams and gnawed them to bits. Skeletons which I had strung on a wire nearly 12 feet above ground, were not exempt from their attacks. After several fruitless attempts they gave up shaking the wire, and winding their tails round it, slid down upon their booty.

Nevertheless we got our fun out of

Right: Andreas Reischek, the Austrian taxidermist, who collected 37 different species of native birds during his five months in Chalky Inlet in 1887. *(A. Reischek)*

Secluded Lake Hector, which Reischek named after Dr Hector. (*J. Hall-Jones*)

them. Rimmer was such a sound sleeper that he did not even wake on one occasion when I fired off a gun at them. Once, however, he could not help sitting up and taking notice. He found a mob of them sitting round his head, gnawing his hair and beard. He shot out of bed as though a tarantula had stung him, got a stick and slew as many of his tormentors as he could."

Stoats became an even greater enemy of the birds than the rats and recently DOC carried out a highly successful stoat-trapping programme on Chalky Island with the aim of re-establishing kakapo there. In 2002, after a 'bumper' breeding season on Codfish Island, DOC transferred 14 kakapo to Chalky Island.

On 20 June the *Stella* called again at Fisherman Bay and the following day Reischek, Rimmer and Caesar were on the open sea heading up the Fiordland coast. (Today there are no obvious remains of Reischek's hut, but a man-made arrangement of stones at the mouth of the river at Fisherman Bay could have been the hearth. Alternatively, a similar one at the back of the sand-dunes.)

Two Fish Freezers

In 1896 William Hanning established a fish freezer, mainly for freezing blue cod, in the NE corner of Fisherman Bay. The station continued to operate until at least 1906, when Hanning died and probably for several years afterwards. William Hanning's son Cyril (known as "Honey") worked at the station and a clearing at Fisherman Bay became known as "Honey's Garden".

The impressive concrete pillars of the wharf, made of local shells and stones, are still there, also the wharf piles, slipway, water race and hut sites.

Above right: ss Stella, in better days, anchored in Milford Sound. (*Burton Bros*)

Right: The rusting hull of the *Stella* in North Port, 1997. The concrete freezing chamber can be seen, aft, on the beach behind the wreck. (*J. Hall-Jones*)

Concrete pillars of the wharf of William Hanning's fishing station at Fisherman Bay, North Port, 1999. (*J. Hall-Jones*)

The other fish freezer in North Port was the hull of the *Stella* at the northern outlet of the harbour. A handsome clipper-bowed steamer in her day, the *ss Stella* was built in Scotland in 1876 for the New Zealand Government for servicing lighthouses. She also delivered mail and took on passengers and we have just seen how she dropped Reischek off at North Port, then picked him up again. The *Stella's* service with the Government ceased in 1889. After that she continued to sail privately in the coastal trade, until 1926 when she was partially dismantled. The hull was used as a freezer base, firstly in Luncheon Cove, then in Fisherman Bay and finally at the northern outlet of North Port. The long slim hull of the fine old steamer can be seen tipped on her side, quietly rusting away. On the beach immediately behind the hull is the old concrete freezing chamber for the storage of fish.

Grono's Cave

In 1905 Captain Harry Roderique of Bluff picked up a piece of slate inside a large cave (known as Grono's Cave) on the Tasman Sea side of Cape Providence. Two separate messages had been scratched on the slate, probably both in 1823:-

Lono
Richard Jones Esq. Owner
John Dawson master
Beware of the Natives plentey
at Preservation

Brig Elizabeth
John Grono Mas
called at this place
the 23rd December
Brooks
Edward Norton

The first message was inscribed by Captain John Dawson of the sealer *Samuel* when he picked up the battered survivors of a *General Gates* sealing gang after their skirmish with the Maori, hence the warning "Beware of the Natives plentey at Preservation".

The second message was left by Captain John Grono, master of the brig *Elizabeth* and was dated "23rd December" (1823). The "Brooks" would be Alexander Books, Grono's son-in-law, who later took over command of the *Elizabeth* when Grono retired from the sea in 1824.

The brig *Elizabeth* (130 tons) was built by Grono at his shipyard on the Hawkesbury River in 1821. Naming the ship after his wife, he launched the *Elizabeth*, "amidst the shouts of a numerous concourse of people. It reflects great credit on the exertions of her owner", the newspaper reported.

On his maiden voyage in the *Elizabeth,* Grono headed for one of his favourite haunts, Chalky Inlet, only to find his anchorage in South Port 'occupied' by a *General Gates* sealing gang. Grono arrested the gang on the rather slim pretext that they were runaway convicts (at least one was), but on his arrival in Sydney he was accused of trying to clear some 'trespassers' off his 'private' sealing grounds and he was ordered to return the gang to Chalky Inlet. Grono made at least two more voyages across to the Fiordland coast in the *Elizabeth* and on what was probably his last voyage, he arrived back in Sydney on 30 March 1824 with a cargo of 5,300 sealskins from the Chalky Inlet area.

John Grono was therefore thoroughly familiar with Chalky Inlet and Grono's Cave. The historian Robert McNab describes Grono's Cave as being "well known as a haunt of seals".

Intrigued with the two messages on the slate and the prospect of discovering the visible remains of a sealing station, I determined to visit Grono's Cave. In May 1972 Leigh Morris, Russell Wall and I flew by amphibian to North Port and landed at "Honey's Garden" in Fisherman Bay. It took us two days to follow Reischek's route through the thick bush to Landing Bay, where we bedded down for the night in paua collector Fred Flutey's hut. (Fred Flutey had told us that he got all his best paua shells for his famous paua house in Bluff from this area.)

The next day was an easy 50 minute walk from Landing Bay across a narrow isthmus to the West Coast, then south along the beach to Grono's Cove, with Grono's Cave at its head.

Grono's Cave proved to be quite the largest and driest cave I have seen on the whole Fiordland coast. The entrance was well protected from the elements by a large mound of rubble in front. We elected to camp inside and were warm and snug in the wildest of storms during the eight days we were there.

Inside there was a large entrance chamber, 7 metres wide and 3 metres high, which had two long offshoot passages extending 27 metres far into the interior. The floor was bone dry but was scattered with paua shells and seal bones, the 'left-overs' of feasts by the former Maori and European cave-dwellers.

At the junction of the two offshoot passages we discovered a large cache of sealskins. They had been deposited in a shallow rectangular shaped pit, 2 x 3 metres, and covered with a layer of ferns, the whole heap being held down by a rectangle of heavy rocks laid around the periphery. The skins had been salted for preservation and were stacked to a depth of 15 centimetres.

Fred Flutey told us that he found two below-knee seaman's boots in the

The historic piece of slate, with messages by Captain Dawson and Captain Grono in 1823, which was found in Grono's Cave in 1905. (*Southland Museum*)

Hut (now demolished) belonging to paua collector Fred Flutey at Landing Bay, 1972. (*J. Hall-Jones*)

The tomb of John and Elizabeth Grono outside Ebenezer Church on the Hawkesbury River. Their son-in-law's name, Captain Alexander Books, is on the opposite side. (*J. Hall-Jones*)

Weather-beaten archway on the wild west coast, across the isthmus from Landing Bay. (*J. Hall-Jones*)

Right: Overgrown mound of rubble that conceals the entrance chamber of Grono's Cave. (*J. Hall-Jones*)

Left: Grono's Cove, with Grono's Cave directly behind the white boulder on the beach. (*J. Hall-Jones*)

cave, also some old bone buttons. During our survey of Grono's Cave and its adjoining caves we found pieces of old hand-blown glass, fragments of leather from a hand-made boot and the cast-iron blade of a skinning knife, all confirming the European occupancy of the caves. We also found strong evidence of prior Maori habitation in the way of seven stone adzes, a greenstone (nephrite) adze, a heavy stone pounder, a paua flick and pieces of plaited flax. There was also a large amount of Maori midden material, shells, fish bones, bird bones and seal bones in all the caves.

At the northern entrance of the cove a rocky point jutted out into the Tasman Sea. 'Sealers Point', as we called it, was only a few minutes walk around the cove from Grono's Cave. We visited the point regularly during our stay, counting 20-30 seals each time, which was by far the largest seal colony that we saw on the whole coast. Also on Sealers Point we found several broken seal bones beside a large rock slab, which would serve well as a skinning table.

Fur seal basking on Sealers Point. (*J. Hall-Jones*)

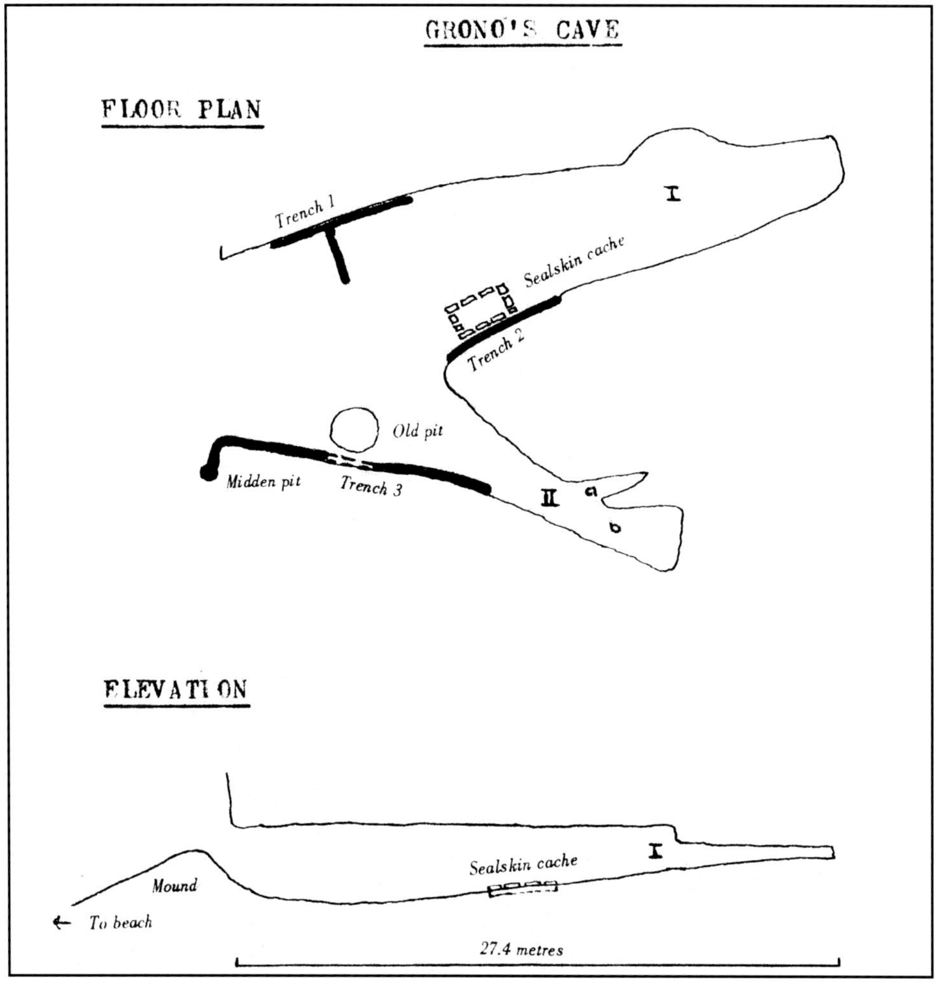

Plan of Grono's Cave. Note mound concealing large entrance chamber, which has two long passages leading off it. Rectangle of rocks around sealskin cache at the beginning of the larger passage. (*Copyright J. Hall-Jones*)

From Lookout Point looking down on Sealers Point and out into the Tasman Sea. (*J. Hall-Jones*)

Left: Some of the Maori artefacts found in Grono's Cave in 1974; three stone adzes and piece of plaited flax. Also a piece of salted sealskin from the sealers' cache. (*J. Hall-Jones*)

Nearby was a rock overhang streaked with black lines of thick soot, such as would be deposited from burning seal fat.

Immediately above Sealers Point was a prominent headland, 'Lookout Point' as we called it. We scrambled up to find that it had been deliberately burnt over and cleared to give a superb 180° uninterrupted view from West Cape in the north to Chalky Island in the south and far out into the Tasman Sea. An ideal lookout for ships coming from Dusky Sound and Chalky Inlet and also from the Tasman Sea. From Lookout Point we could see a cleared channel running in through the rocks of Grono's Cove, leading right to the beach below Grono's Cave – a lane which had obviously been cleared to bring whaleboats in through the rock-studded landing. At the back of the beach, immediately behind the channel, was a very solid old log and two pieces of plank with hand-beaten rivets. This

would be where the whaleboats were hauled ashore.

From all our findings we could now piece together a mental picture of early Maori using the cave as a base for hunting a wide range of animal species over many years. Sealing gangs landing by longboats at the head of Grono's Cove and living in Grono's Cave while they slaughtered and skinned the seals of the seal colony on Sealers Point; salting the skins and caching them inside the bone dry cave, all the time keeping a watch mounted on Lookout Point for the mother ship returning to pick up the cache and the sealing gang. Most of the skins would be exported in this way, but as to who left the last cache in Grono's Cave nobody knows. Perhaps it was John Grono, or his son-in-law Alexander Books. Or was it some sealer unknown? Whatever, Grono's Cove is the only place on the Fiordland coast where the whole workings of a sealing station can be visualised.

The survey completed, the three troglodytes departed the shelter of Grono's Cave and carried on along the beach to Cape Providence. As we approached the cape the setting sun lit up the strikingly white cliffs of Chalky Island. Entering the tidal tunnel at the very tip of the cape (Boultbee's "Cave Point") I was somewhat startled to be confronted with an old human thigh bone lying inside. Maybe it belonged to one of the sealers whose boat was wrecked on the "dangerous rocks of Cave Point", as recorded by Boultbee. Exiting from the tunnel into Landing Bay we were greeted by the friendly light of Puysegur Point which illuminated our way along the beach to Fred's hut, where we stayed for the night.

The following day we arrived back at Fisherman Bay, all prepared for our arranged flight out the next day. The evening was quiet and still. Too quiet, the quiet before a storm. For five days it rained and rained and rained, until it started to hail! We soon ran out of food. On the third day we shared a small tin of jam between us, then there was nothing. We stayed in our sleeping bags to conserve our heat and energy. Then on the sixth day of our ordeal, we heard the roar of the amphibian's engine, the most welcome sound that the three of us had ever heard in our lives! Safely home we found that each of us had lost 4-5 kilograms weight. Wisely my wife, an ex-district nurse, fed us lightly on bowls of nourishing soup. She says that she will never forget our appearances – pale, wasted and slow in our reactions – we were suffering from hypothermia.

Left: Mother ship landing a sealing gang in a wild remote rocky cove. (*J. Cumpston*)

CHAPTER 9

Caswell's for Marble

Caswell's Harbour is one of those wild bold-looking sea views so common in New Zealand.
John Boultbee, 1826

In 1826 John Boultbee's sealing gang landed on sea-swept Styles Island at the entrance to Caswell Sound.

"Caswell's Harbour", writes Boultbee, "is one of those wild bold looking sea views so common in New Zealand. It is pretty spacious and on each side the mountains rise suddenly up to a considerable height. They are for the most part covered with trees, such as iron wood [rata], pine [rimu] etc. The extensive distant back view consists of snow-topped and cloud [capped] mountains. A small island [Styles Island] lays near the entrance of the harbour where we hauled our boat up." (For anyone who has seen the sea breaking on the rugged rocks of Styles Island,

Right: A fine painting by C. H. Howorth of the entrance of Caswell Sound, 1883. Styles Island on right. (*Hocken Library*)

this would seem an impossible feat, but there is a smoother landing on the inner aspect of the island.)

Commander Richards of the *Acheron* survey was also impressed by the rugged mountains of Caswell Sound. In 1851 he climbed a peak on the south side of the fjord (?Fleetwood Peak) to describe the "vast sea of mountains of every possible variety of shape and ruggedness". With the mist floating far below on the fjord "the harbour appeared to be no more than an insignificant stream".

Caswell Sound appears to be another of John Grono's names. The strange name of Mt Tanilba for one of the Caswell Sound mountains gives us a clue. Lieutenant William Caswell was the owner of Tanilba Station in New South Wales and apparently Caswell and Grono knew each other.

The Promised Land

During his survey of Lake Te Anau surveyor James McKerrow set off up the Middle Fiord in high hopes of becoming the first European to see the West Coast from Lake Te Anau. On New Year's Day 1863 McKerrow and his assistant, John Goldie, pushed their way up the slopes of Mt Pisgah at the head of the Fiord, but alas the west was shrouded in fog. Thoroughly soaked they returned to their camp without seeing the coast. For three consecutive days they climbed the peak, but each time they were thwarted by either rain or fog.

Rocky Styles Island at the entrance of Caswell Sound, where John Boultbee's sealing gang landed in 1826. (*J. Hall-Jones*)

Left: Surveyor James McKerrow who climbed Mt Pisgah in 1863 and saw Caswell Sound lying to the west. (*Hocken Library*)

Facing page: McKerrow's view of Caswell Sound showing this long narrow fjord, with Styles Island lying in the entrance. Also the Stillwater River entering the head of the fjord. (*DOC*)

With their damper running low and their meat coming to life they decided upon one last attempt. The day dawned with a light fog which gradually lifted as they climbed. Then, "there to the west lay Caswell Sound with the island at its mouth [Styles Island] and the surf beating on the rocks". McKerrow named the mountain Pisgah, "from which Moses saw the long expected and promised land on a much more important occasion".

Mackinnon Discovers a Route

It is not generally known that a year before Quintin Mackinnon made his momentous first crossing of the

Below: The explorer Quintin Mackinnon who discovered an overland route to Caswell Sound in 1887. (*Hocken Library*)

From the foot of Lake Marchant looking towards the mouth of the Large Burn, where Mackinnon finished his journey. *(J. Hall-Jones)*

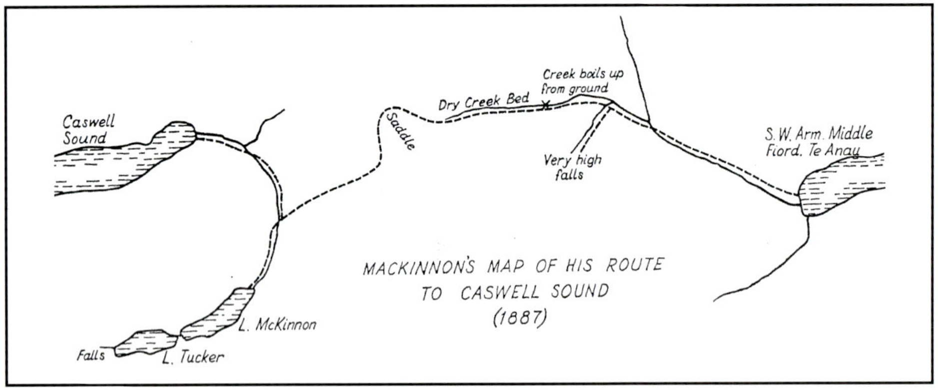

Mackinnon's map, 1887. Note how he labels Lake Marchant as "Caswell Sound". Also his two separate lakes for Lake Mackinnon. *(Copyright J Hall-Jones)*

famous Mackinnon Pass, he discovered a route through to Caswell Sound from Lake Te Anau. Mackinnon had been commissioned by C. W. Adams, the Chief Surveyor of Otago, to discover a route through to the West Coast from Lake Te Anau, and in 1887 Mackinnon and George Tucker set off from the head of the Middle Fiord of the lake. Following up the Doon River they crossed a saddle and descended into the Large Burn Valley. They came to a long lake with a narrow constriction in its middle, which made Mackinnon think that it was two separate lakes and he named them Lakes Mackinnon and Tucker. Continuing on, the two explorers arrived at a long sheet of water which they thought was Caswell Sound and Mackinnon marked it as such on his map. Actually they had arrived at the head of Lake Marchant, which is almost at sealevel, and Caswell Sound is only one hour's easy walk from the foot of this lake.

Mackinnon reported his success in finding a route through to the West Coast to Adams and it was probably because of this that he was given the job of blazing a track up the Clinton Valley, in the hope of finding a route through to Milford Sound. A job that was to result in the spectacular discovery of the Mackinnon Pass and the route of the now famous Milford Track.

Remains of whaleboat at the marble mine landing, 1978. *(K. Morrison)*

The Marble Mine

Although Quintin Mackinnon has previously been credited with the discovery of the white marble lode in Caswell Sound, the fact that he only got as far as the head of Lake Marchant disproves this.

In 1874 a licence was issued to Turnley, Smith & Co. to mine the white marble at Caswell Sound for the manufacture of statuary. Nothing was done about it until 1881, when the government geologist Alexander McKay was sent to report on the company's prospects for mining the marble lode. McKay was landed from *ss Kennedy* at the site of the marble outcrop, about a third of the way inside the fjord on the south side. "The white statuary marble towards which the energies of the company are directed", reported McKay, "shows at the water's edge. [From what can be] seen from its surface the marble is sound and free from joints, and could be quarried in blocks of any size required." Penetrating the marble outcrop from below was a marble cave and McKay found that its "entrance was choked with several blocks of marble". The quarry, being an open cast mine, McKay concluded that it could be worked easily. But he "did not consider it within his province" to comment upon the profitability of such a venture.

The Caswell Sound Mining Company decided to proceed and early in 1882 a party sailed from Dunedin under the charge of a mining manager, A. H. Malcolm. By February the miners had quarried enough white marble for the company's secretary to sail to Melbourne with six tons of marble blocks for the manufacture of statuary.

However, the extravagant claims of the company contrasted strangely with the four little weather-board huts at Caswell Sound. The company had run into difficulty in selling their product. The beautiful white marble, as seen on the surface, had a coarse internal structure which made it fragmentary and no use for statuary.

When the *Tarawera* passed the mine in 1883 the passengers could see "two or three weather-board huts in a clearing with blocks of stone nearby". The two eminent geologists aboard, Sir James Hector and Sir Julius von Haast, went ashore and found "what had been opened [in the quarry] was as yet too shattered and broken [to be

Rusting roof of hut at the marble mine settlement, 1992. (*J. Hall-Jones*)

Left: The open cast marble mine quarry, 1992. *Right:* Entrance to the marble cave where cut blocks of marble were found. (*J. Hall-Jones*)

of use]". By 1887, when Andreas Reischek visited the quarry on board the *Stella*, he found that all work had ceased and the settlement was deserted.

In 1992 I visited the quarry as part of a DOC. survey of historic sites. We landed at the tiny rocky cove below the settlement. There, at the head of the cove, were the rotting bows of two clinker built whaleboats and remains of an old iron winch. Scrambling up the hillside above the landing we came to the collapsed remnants of four wooden huts, their rusting corrugated iron roofs lying flat on the ground. Continuing on we came to the site of the quarry workshop, with some old iron rods lying around. From there we descended along an old track towards the sea to arrive at the open cast marble quarry. Below the quarry, just above sealevel, was McKay's cave with blocks of marble inside the entrance.

Ranger Kim Morrison visited the marble cave in 1978 and found a large wooden box inside, which he concluded had been used for sledging the cut marble blocks outside. He also found "several squared marble blocks (about 1 x 1 x 1 metres) on the shore below", ready for loading onto ships.

mv Alert landing stores at the head of Caswell Sound for the New Zealand-American wapiti expedition in 1949. (*National Publicity Studio*)

Moored in the mouth of the Stillwater River at the head of Caswell Sound. (*J. Hall-Jones*)

Here then are the visible remains of the failed marble venture in Caswell Sound in the 1880s.

New Zealand-American Wapiti Survey

During World War II an American, Colonel John K. Howard, became interested in the American wapiti herd that had been liberated in George Sound in 1905. Colonel Howard's interest was not confined to hunting and in 1947 he promoted a comparative study of the wapiti herd in New Zealand with the mother herd in America. He returned to New Zealand that year and with the assistance of experienced wapiti hunters and wildlife officers defined the main wapiti breeding block as lying between Caswell and Bligh Sounds to the west and the North and Middle Fiords of Lake Te Anau to the east. The scientists had only three weeks in the field and concluded that if a proper study was to be undertaken, then they would need a much longer time and a much larger expedition.

For the subsequent 1949 combined survey, Colonel Howard invited Olaus Murie, who had made an extensive study of wapiti in America, to join the expedition. Captain Alex Black's *mv Alert* was charted to run fortnightly supply trips to the two beachheads at Caswell and George Sounds. In early

Left: Looking down on the Stillwater Valley, where Baughan Wisely saw two kakapo in 1947. The prominent peak on the centre skyline is Mt Irene. (*J. Hall-Jones*)

Right: Cookhouse at the expedition's main base camp in the Stillwater Valley, 1949. (*N.Z. Govt Studio*)

Below left: The restored 1949 expedition hut at the head of Caswell Sound, 2000. (*J. Hall-Jones*)

January 1949 Colonel Howard and the field party sailed from Bluff in the *Alert* for Caswell Sound.

The stores were unloaded on the beach at the head of Caswell Sound, where a small hut was built. From there the stores were backpacked about a kilometre to the foot of Lake Marchant, where they were loaded onto flat-bottomed dinghys with outboard motors for transport up the Stillwater River to its junction with Expectation Stream, where the main base camp was established. From this base camp field parties ranged over the large Stillwater watershed and right across to George Sound. Then on 7 April, the expedition shifted to the George Sound hut, which became the base until early May, when most of the party departed via the George Sound track to the Middle Fiord of Lake Te Anau.

In his summary of the findings of the expedition, Olaus Murie concluded that there was "some evidence" that the New Zealand wapiti herd was cross-breeding with the red deer population. The work of the expedition was not confined to a study of wapiti and the overall report by A. L. Poole includes a number of important scientific papers on the flora, fauna and geology of the whole area. Of particular interest two kakapo were "encountered" in the bush in the Stillwater Valley by zoologist Baughan Wisely, one on "a leading ridge" and the other at an "altitude of 600 metres".

CHAPTER 10

George's Harbour

George's Harbour is a deep inlet surrounded by high mountains covered with trees.
John Boultbee, 1826

John Boultbee was one of the sealers aboard the brig *Elizabeth* (formerly Grono's) when Captain Kent sailed her out of Sydney on 14 March 1826 to set down four sealing gangs on the Fiordland coast. On 5 April the *Elizabeth* anchored in "George's Harbour" (George Sound) where all four sealing boats and provisions for six months were landed. Boultbee's boat and two others were to work the coast north to Milford Sound and as far as Open Bay Islands, 150 kilometres away. They were then to sail south to Dusky Sound where Captain Kent would pick them up in the *Elizabeth*.

Looking down on George Sound from Saddle Hill. (*B. Miles*)

Before departing George Sound, Boultbee recorded the first ever description of this fjord:

"George's Harbour is a deep inlet, surrounded by high mountains covered with trees and when we anchored at the head of the cove [Anchorage Cove – *see later*] we could barely see the sun above, two hours in the day, so that the air was cold and chilly."

Taking enough provisions for six weeks, three muskets and a dog, Boultbee's boat and the other two whaleboats headed north to seal the coast for 150 kilometres. A few weeks later they were back at "George's Harbour" on their way south for their arranged rendezvous at Dusky Sound.

> "In the Evening we arrived safe at George's Harbour. Here we all got a change of clothes, & made a huge blazing fire in one of the huts, where we hung our large iron pot, & boiled some tea; this, & our substantial but coarse food – pork & cakes baked in the ashes, refreshed us, and after a few songs, corresponding with the characters & manners of the parties, we wrapped ourselves up in our blankets, careless how the world went & free from those anxieties for the future, which are the bane of human comfort.
>
> In the night we had a very heavy gale, & we were a good deal pleased that we were safe & snug on shore; the rocks were tumbling down the high precipices which bounded the small level flat on which we were living, carrying away stumps and bushes before them. In the morning we found our boats turned over & covered with sand, & the seal clubs that we had stuck in the ground & were 3 feet above the surface were covered entirely up."

The fact that their boats were turned over and covered with sand, pinpoints the sealers huts as being sited at Anchorage Cove at the head of the first reach of George Sound and not the very head of the sound, as supposed by the Begg brothers in their biography of John Boultbee. There is no sign of sand at the head of George Sound, which is very much a rock and boulder beach. In total contrast, at Anchorage Cove there is a very large sandy beach at the mouth of George River, with an excellent flat behind for the sealers to build their huts.

The sandy beach at Anchorage Cove where the sealers' boats were "turned over and covered with sand". *(J. Hall-Jones)*

Anchorage Cove would also give the sealers a far better access to the open sea, instead of having to haul all the way to the head of sound, 20 kilometres in from the sea.

Boultbee's boat was "weather bound for three weeks" in "George's Harbour" before they could "launch and set off the Southward". Before doing so Boultbee gives a hint in his journal of his superior education to his fellow sealers, most of whom were illiterate; something which we have suspected already from his lively style of writing and his perceptive observations.

"You will see, my friends, I had now become an altered person & changed from the delicate youth to about as rough a piece of goods as ever weathered the wide world. Notwithstanding I was as hardy & robust as most people, there was a something about me, which caused my boatmates to suspect I was a degree or two above their level, & I was often amused at their remarks. One day, as I was sitting writing, two or three of the crew observed 'he is a regular *scholard,* & keeps a log of all that is going on'. One said 'I think he must be some *swell*'s son, & has spent his money, its a pity such like chaps should come to this;' but he reckoned we were all born and not buried, & it might happen, he someday or other should have his turn in the balance. With this piece of philosophic reflection, he comforted himself, trusting to Fortune for his advancement or downfall. But to Jack, a chew of tobacco was the 'ne plus ultra' of his wishes and desires."

It is now known that John Boultbee was born in Nottinghamshire, the youngest son of a captain in the Royal Marines and later an estate manager for the Earl of Maclesfield. The young John had a nanny, a schoolmaster, then went to boarding school, from which he ran away regularly. A born wanderer he travelled to Brazil at the age of 17, then emigrated to Tasmania where he later joined Captain Kent's sealing gang. His *Journal of a Rambler*, as he called it, is a unique and highly valuable record of sealing on the Fiordland coast, written by a well-educated and observant young man. Although culturally different from his fellow sealers, he got on well with them, "we were on good-terms with one another and nothing but goodwill was manifested towards me".

Eventually Boultbee's boat got away from "George's Harbour", but as they headed south, Boultbee was tipped out at one of their landings. "On our way we hauled up at different places, at one of which, the boat in which I was, upset in a surf & threw me out, & I was nearly run over by the boat as she made a sheer on towards the beach."

After landing on Styles Island in "Caswell's Harbour" they continued on to "Thomson's Sound", which Boultbee describes as "a passage between an island [Secretary Island] & the Main, extending about 18 miles in length, & running in a serpentine direction. The scenery is very picturesque, comprising small woody islands, arms of the sea branching off & in different directions & high hanging woody eminences. In going through the Sound, we shot some seal in the water. In the evening we arrived at a small harbour at the S. end of the Sound." (Blanket Bay, now a fishermen's base, the Blanket Bay 'Hotel'.)

From Doubtful Sound the whaleboat carried on to Dusky Sound and Chalky Inlet, as we have seen already and met up with Captain Kent, who was "disappointed" to find that they had only 290 sealskins with them. Restocking with provisions and new clothing, the "rambler" continued on in the whaleboat to the sealing grounds of Foveaux Strait and Stewart Island.

A Good Anchorage

Like the sealers before them, the *Acheron* surveyors also found Anchorage Cove "a good anchorage" and named it so. "With north-west gales a swell sets in, but by hauling over to the north shore of Anchorage Cove and securing to the trees a vessel will be in smooth water. The head of this cove is a sandy beach", noted Commander Richards, "through which flows a rapid river [George River]."

"George Sound is surrounded by mountains, of the most rugged and precipitous character", describes Richards, "with striking and perpendicular ranges on either side, nearly 5,000 feet high. At the head of the sound is a small basin, and about 200 feet above the sea is an extensive lake [Lake Alice], whose superfluous waters run into [the basin] by an easy descent [Alice Falls] down the mountain side, causing a considerable outset in the harbour."

Lake Alice and the Alice Falls at the head of George Sound. From Saddle Hill. (*J. Hall-Jones*)

Looking down on Lake Katherine from Marguerite Peaks. (*J. Hall-Jones*)

A Very Passable Route

In October 1899 Richard Henry and Robert Murrell set out from the Middle Fiord of Lake Te Anau in a determined bid to find a route through to George Sound. Fashioning a canoe out of a log they paddled their way to the head of Lake Hankinson. After crossing Lake Thomson in their portable canvas boat they continued up the main valley to discover a low pass leading to the west. Ascending the pass they climbed its northern flank, "an easy climb", to reach the summit of Mt Henry, where they "built a cairn and left their names and the date".

From the summit of Mt Henry they could see George Sound and a large valley leading down from their pass to the head of the Sound. They had found "a very passable route" to George Sound, as Henry reported to Chief Surveyor C. W. Adams in his delightful pithy style. Returning to the pass, which they called "George's Saddle", they descended the large valley and traversed round Lake Katherine to reach the boulder beach at the head of George Sound (now the site of the DOC hut).

Although Henry "didn't see" Lake Alice at the head of the Alice Falls, he copied this onto his map from the *Acheron* chart, with the comment (correctly) "probably too far south". The two lakes, Katherine, and Alice,

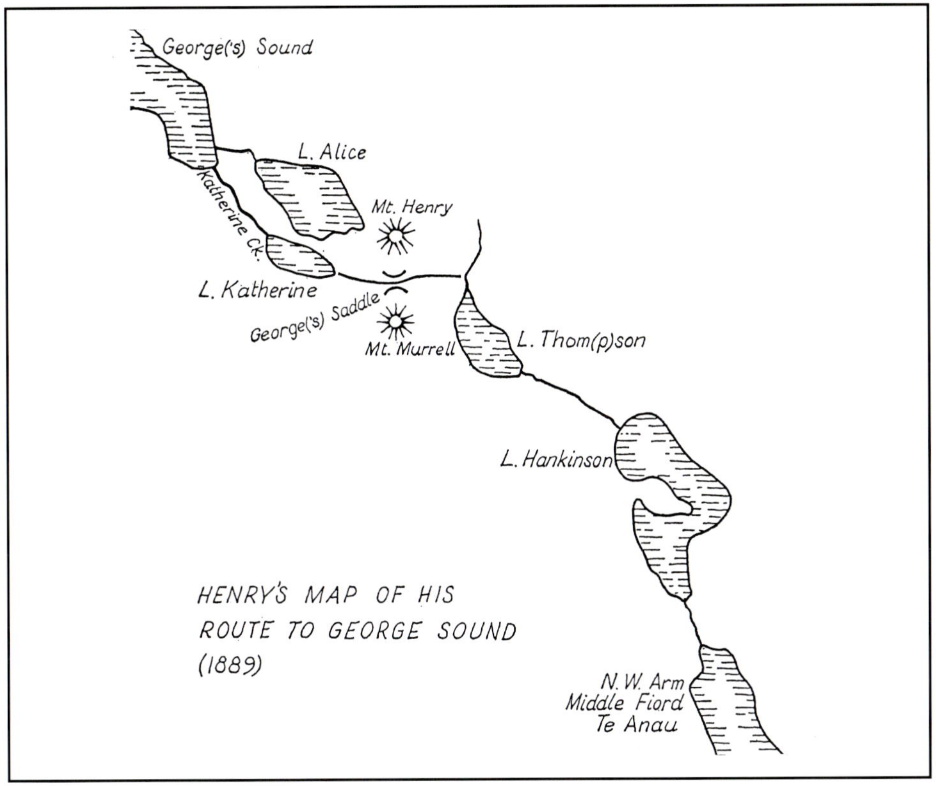

Diagram from Henry's map. (*Copyright, J. Hall-Jones*)

On Henry Pass, Henry's "George's Saddle". Mt Murrell and Marguerite Peaks on skyline. (*J. Hall-Jones*)

Henry named after Mrs Katherine Alice Melland of Te Anau Downs Station where he worked from time to time. Describing Lake Katherine to Mrs Melland later, Henry told her how it was "crowded with wild duck and teal of different kinds; grebe and other fowl. The birds had never seen a human being, gun or dog, so they had no fear and allowed us to come as close as we liked, without offering to fly."

In Henry's report to Adams he also proposed the name Mt Murrell, on the opposite side of "George's Saddle" from Mt Henry, "after my very good mate". He hoped that the Chief Surveyor had no objection to these names "as there are mountains enough for everyone up here[!] I have proved that a very passable route [to George Sound] exists and I think you will be pleased with my discovery. I could have blazed a track right through [to the Sound], but I had an idea that a surveyor might choose a better grade. [From Mt Henry] many landmarks can be seen to connect surveys. I am at your service to take over your surveyor. I hope that you will send someone soon." The whole journey had taken 26 days, but as Henry points out they were exploring and track-cutting and were also held up by bad weather and having to build a canoe.

In February 1890 surveyor Frank Coote of Melbourne arrived at Te Anau to survey the George Sound track. Guided by Henry, the party took only five days for the round trip, surveying all the way. Henry's proposed names were accepted for the map and in honour of Henry's discovery of the pass, his modest naming of "George's Saddle" was changed to Henry Pass.

It took another seven years before a track-cutting contract was let and boats placed on Lakes Hankinson and Thomson. Today the George Sound track remains one of the most rewarding but challenging tracks in the Fiordland National Park.

American elk (wapiti) in its homeland in the Rockies, photographed grazing right beside the main highway. (*J. Hall-Jones*)

Wapiti Released

In 1905 the government steamer *Hinemoa* landed 18 American elk at the head of George Sound and released them into the wilds of Fiordland. Of the original shipment of 20, ten had been gifted by President "Teddy" Roosevelt, a keen sportsman, and ten had been purchased by the New Zealand Government, but two of them died on the voyage. Better known in America as American elk, the New Zealand Government chose to call the deer by their original Indian name – wapiti.

To allow the herd to become established, the Government made it illegal to shoot wapiti, a bar which remained in place up till 1923. Within a year of their release a wapiti bull was shot illegally by a lawyer, J. Park, on the shore of Lake Katherine.

In 1921 the Southland Acclimatisation Society sent its Te Anau ranger, Charlie Evans, to report on the herd. Accompanied by H. Beer, Evans started out on the George Sound track, carrying a canoe across to Lake Hankinson, so that they could reach its head. "On our way to Lake Thomson", reports Evans,

Left: Ranger Charlie Evans who reported on the wapiti herd in 1921. (*D. B. Banwell*)

"we got our first glimpse of one, which may be described as a wapiti bull with antlers. The colour was white from under the mouth to the breast, while the back view showed the colouring of a Jersey bull". (Evans is describing the typically pale rump of a wapiti.) As they ascended Henry Pass they came across a well-defined track, which Evans concluded had been formed by wapiti, "as a means of travel from George Sound to the feed in the valley on the Te Anau". The wapiti had discovered Henry's "very passable route" from George Sound to the pastures of the lakes on the Te Anau side. Unfortunately it was "snowing

14-pointer wapiti stag shot at the head of Lake Katherine by Vivian Donald in 1923, the first wapiti shot under licence. (*D.B. Banwell*)

Paddling the old flat-bottomed punt on Lake Hankinson, 1956. (*J. Hall-Jones*)

heavily" when Evans reached the top of Henry Pass and he was unable to proceed any further. He was able to conclude that the wapiti herd was spreading and that at least 20 beasts were thriving on the Te Anau side of Henry Pass.

The Acclimatisation Society showed its ranger's report to the Prime Minister, William Massey, when he visited Invercargill in 1922 and suggested that a season be opened to hunt the wapiti. The request was granted in 1923 and Vivian Donald of Masterton and Leslie Murrell of Manapouri were each issued with a licence to shoot a trophy bull. Landing at the head of George Sound with Leslie Murrell in April 1923, Vivian Donald shot a fine 14-pointer bull at the head of Lake Katherine – the first wapiti shot legally under licence in New Zealand. Returning later to the lake, Donald shot a second bull, a 15-pointer, but not as large as his first one. They moved to Caswell Sound where Murrell shot a bull, an 11-pointer, on the edge of Lake Marchant. "We now had a bull each and one for the Government", recounts an elated Donald.

With the spread of the wapiti south to Caswell Sound and east to Lake Te Anau, the herd was obviously thriving. The hunt for trophies was on, with trophy-hunters being attracted from all round New Zealand and even from overseas. The story of these trophy hunts has been meticulously researched and documented by Bruce Banwell in his book *Wapiti in New Zealand*.

Kakapo Tracks at George Sound

Although Charlie Evans had seen numerous kakapo on his 1921 wapiti survey, by the early 1930s wapiti hunters were noticing that kakapo numbers were falling off quite dramatically. The lethal stoats were getting at them. Baughan Wisely's "encounter" with two kakapo in the Stillwater Valley in 1947 was the last report of a kakapo sighting in the whole Caswell-George Sounds region.

One of our 'Kontiki' lilo-rafts at the head of George Sound. (*J. Hall-Jones*)

Lilo-rafting our gear across the head of George Sound. (*J. Hall-Jones*)

Kakapo Castle on Saddle Hill. The track and bowl system was on the summit skyline. (*J. Hall-Jones*)

The 50 metre kakapo pathway found on Saddle Hill in 1956. (*J. Hall-Jones*)

Keen to follow up Baughan's last sighting, Alistair Carey, Lieutenant Tom Couzens and I discussed this with Baughan and he recommended Saddle Hill, a steep-walled, isolated mountain between George and Caswell Sounds as a likely final retreat of the beleaguered bird. To get to Saddle Hill we would have to traverse the route of the 'track' to George Sound, then ascend a steep ridge from the Sound to begin our search.

In 1956 when we started the trip the 'track' was unused, heavily overgrown and wind-fallen and without any wire bridges to cross some quite major rivers. After being dumped by *mv Tawera* at the head of the Middle Fiord, we crossed to Lake Hankinson to discover that the 'boat' was a rectangular, flat-bottomed punt, without any oars! Fashioning two crude 'paddles' out of manuka poles and planking, we launched the crazy craft into the water. With the assistance of a 'parka sail' we paddled our way slowly but surely to the head of the lake. Lake Thomson was one stage worse. There was no boat at all and no wire bridge to cross the raging river at its outlet. So we had to traverse the bluffs on the wrong side of the lake from the 'track'. Crossing Henry Pass we descended to Lake Katherine, but there the river was in flood, so for the second time we had to take to the bluffs on the wrong side of the lake, without any track. When the cliffs became impossible to negotiate we lashed our lilos together with a framework of saplings and proceeded 'Kontiki style' to the end of the lake. We eventually reached the sanctuary of the DOC. hut at George Sound and three days later ornithologist Brian Reid flew in by amphibian with all the supplies for our Saddle Hill expedition. Loading the supplies on to our Kontiki rafts, we convoyed them across the bay to the foot of the steep ridge leading up to Saddle Hill.

As we ascended the ridge we got our first view of the impressive cliffs of Saddle Hill, 'Kakapo Castle', a perfect retreat for an embattled bird. Arriving at the foot of the leading ridge of Saddle Hill Alistair began poking among some boulders. There, to his (and our) excitement, he found the remains of a kakapo (which was later confirmed by Ron Scarlett of the Canterbury Museum). The hunt was on! We ascended the ridge to about 1,100 metres above sealevel,

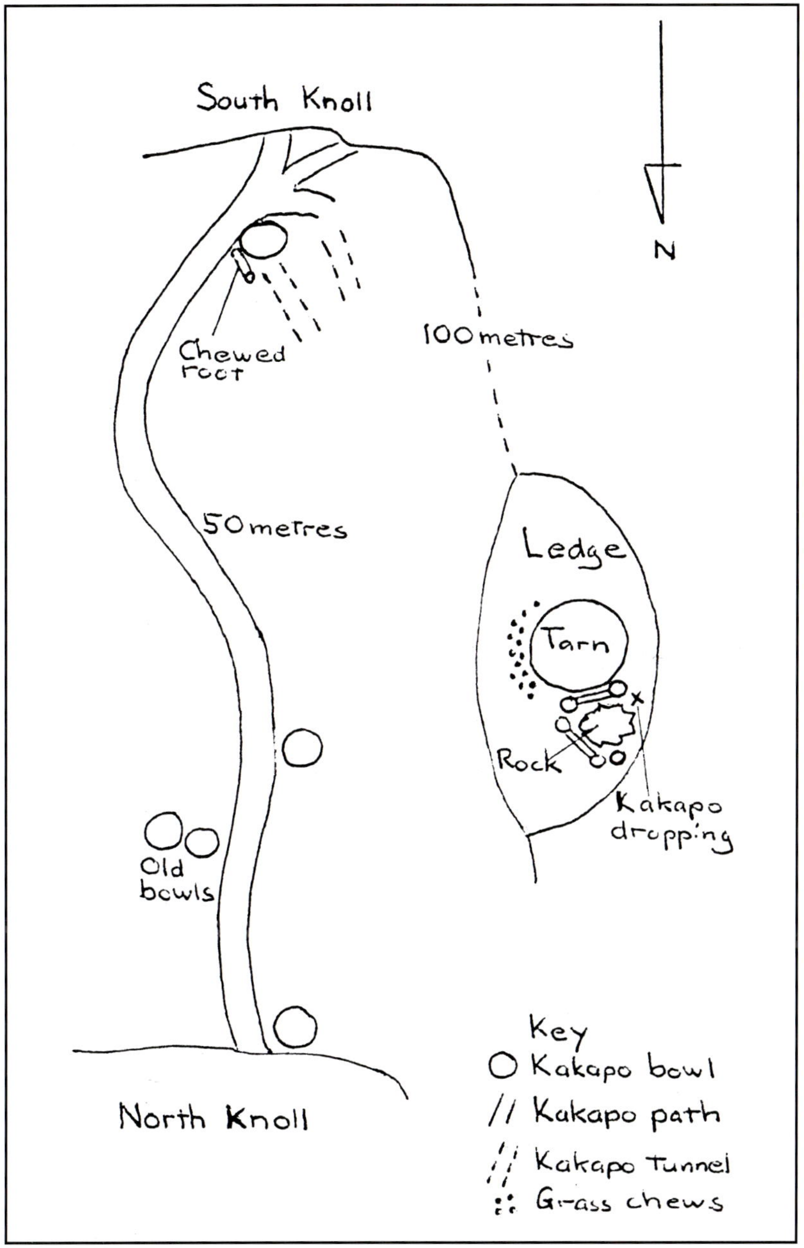

Diagram of the track and bowl systems found on Saddle Hill in 1956. (*Copyright J. Hall-Jones*)

where much to our astonishment we suddenly came upon a well-defined 'pathway' linking two knolls about 50 metres apart. The whole 50 metre 'garden path' (average width 35cm) was noticeably clean and tidy with closely cropped and sharply defined edges. Along the grass verges were five bowl-shaped depressions. Three of these (display) bowls appeared to have been used recently and one had a root which had been nibbled from below. The knolls at either end of the pathway offered extensive panoramic views of George Sound to the north and the Stillwater Valley to the south. The track and bowl system was superbly sited to project boom calls in either direction over a wide ranging area.

On the west side of the pathway, tunnels led steeply down through low stunted scrub to a tiny tarn perched on a rock ledge 100 metres below. Descending to the tarn we discovered another track and bowl system around a rock outcrop. At the edge of the tarn we found a mass of the typically rolled grass chews of kakapo. Also a characteristically coiled grass dropping of kakapo. The whole rock ledge with its tiny tarn was poised on the brink of a great precipice, rendering it safe from any approach to Kakapo Castle by stoats from the valley below.

Excited with our discoveries we slept out that night, keeping a vigil in the precincts of Kakapo Castle, but disappointingly no kakapo were seen or heard.

One evening during our 12-day stay in the area, a shadow swept low over our campfire. The bird had a rapid wing beat and emitted a strange maniacal 'laugh', a sound which none of us had ever heard before. We concluded that this may well have been the very rare laughing owl (*Sceloglaux albifacies*) and interestingly in my follow up research I came across a report by K. Sutherland, a thoroughly reliable witness, that he had observed a laughing owl at close range at Lake Thomson in 1930.

It was fascinating during the research to come across a sketch in 1863 by John Buchanan (the botanist aboard the *Matilda Hayes*) of "Kakapo tracks on a mountain, 3,000 feet above George Sound". The kakapo tracks as drawn by Buchanan had a striking resemblance to the track and bowl system that we had discovered. Like ours, they were on a leading ridge above the Sound and were at the same altitude. Buchanan's "Kakapo tracks" were on the leading ridge of Nita Peaks, on the opposite side of the Katherine Valley from Saddle Hill.

We reported our kakapo finds to the Wildlife Department, but nothing happened until 1960 when wildlife officer Marshall Small of Queenstown invited me to join him and Ralph Adams on an expedition into Tutoko Valley, Milford Sound, where the booming of kakapo had been reported. In 1960 we tramped to the

Male kakapo displaying in a bowl. (*DOC*)

Left: From the kakapo pathway looking down on the kakapo ledge and tarn where another track and bowl system was found. (*J. Hall-Jones*)

Right: John Buchanan's sketch of the kakapo tracks he found on a ridge above George Sound in 1863. Lake Alice below. (*Buchanan papers*)

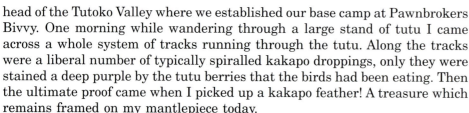

head of the Tutoko Valley where we established our base camp at Pawnbrokers Bivvy. One morning while wandering through a large stand of tutu I came across a whole system of tracks running through the tutu. Along the tracks were a liberal number of typically spiralled kakapo droppings, only they were stained a deep purple by the tutu berries that the birds had been eating. Then the ultimate proof came when I picked up a kakapo feather! A treasure which remains framed on my mantlepiece today.

The following year Ralph Adams returned to the valley with cage-traps and captured a male kakapo. More kakapo were captured in Tutoko Valley and later in Sinbad Gully, below Mitre Peak, but unfortunately all the Fiordland birds turned out to be males. It was only after the kakapo were rediscovered on Stewart Island in 1977 that females were caught and the whole highly successful DOC programme to "save the kakapo" really took off.

In 1989 I returned to the scene of our 1956 kakapo finds with another companion, Bruce Miles. This time we took a 'shortcut' from Henry Pass straight along the tops of Marguerite Peaks to Saddle Hill. Thirty years on, the kakapo pathway was still definable, but its neat and tidy character had changed completely. The edges were no longer closely trimmed and cropped and had become overgrown with grass and shrubs. All five display bowls had become completely overgrown and could no longer be distinguished. Likewise the display bowls on the ledge below had disappeared and there were no longer any signs of kakapo chews or droppings.

The Saddle Hill track and bowl arena for kakapo to boom and display had obviously become disused. Sadly I concluded Kakapo Castle had become deserted.

CHAPTER 11

The Two Monarchs of Charles Sound

As we climbed up to the saddle the top of a new peak began to loom up in the U of the saddle like a mighty foresight of a gun; a most impressive and exciting experience.
Baughan Wisely, 1953

As Dieter and I flew into Charles Sound with our seakayak we passed over the two great monarchs of Western Fiordland, Mt Irene (1,879 metres) and Coronation Peak (1,765 metres), which dominate the heads of the two arms of Charles Sound. The flight had a special meaning for me because almost half a century ago I had been a member of the Canterbury Museum expeditions which had explored and mapped this whole area, naming the beautifully coned Coronation Peak which overlooks the Gold Arm of Charles Sound and the great Irene River which flows down from Mt Irene into the head of the Emelius Arm.

Descending to the helicopter pad in the island-studded Gold Arm, we set out to explore Charles Sound in our seakayak and hopefully ascend the large Irene River.

A comparatively short fjord, Charles Sound is Y-shaped with its two narrow arms, Emelius and Gold, probing eastwards towards Mt Irene and

Below left: The great rock bastion of Mt Irene (1,879 m.), the highest mountain in Western Fiordland. Fog filling the Irene River Valley and the Emelius Arm of Charles Sound on left. (*J. Hall-Jones*)

Below right: The cone of Coronation Peak (1,765 m.), the second highest mountain in Western Fiordland. Fog lying in the Gold Arm of Charles Sound on right. (*J. Hall-Jones*)

Twin waterfalls at the head of Gold Arm. (*J. Hall-Jones*)

Coronation Peak. The Sound was named after Captain Charles McLaren of the *Sydney Cove*, which was sealing there in 1810. But who on earth was Emelius and was gold ever found there?

No Gold in Gold Arm

Mention the word gold to any old goldminer and his eyes will light up and his panning hands will begin to twitch. But he would be wasting his time in Gold Arm because no gold has ever been found there, not a single grain. Why then did Captain Stokes give it the name of Gold Arm? Maybe it was after the strikingly coloured golden moss on a huge rock buttress in this arm, or perhaps after the golden toetoes at the mouth of the Irene River. But no, the reason was to prove far more devious than that.

From a chance reading of Charlotte Godley's *Letters from Early New*

Facing page: Coronation Peak towering high above the wooded islets of Gold Arm, Charles Sound. A fine painting by Jonathan White. (*Courtesy Jonathan White*)

Zealand I learned that Captain Stokes befriended Colonel Charles Gold of the Yorkshire Regiment while the *Acheron* was based in Wellington. The combination of the name Charles with the unusual surname, Gold, registered and left me wondering if Stokes was linking the colonel's name with the *Acheron's* survey of Charles Sound. Described as a "pleasant gentlemanly soldier" the colonel and the captain got on well together and doubtless the regimental balls were popular with the officers of the *Acheron*.

Stokes was genuinely puzzled by the naming of Charles Sound and would wish to name a feature in honour of their genial host in Wellington. As if to clinch the theory a little research revealed that Colonel Charles Gold's second Christian name was Emilius (spelt with an 'i' and not an 'e'), giving us the origin of Stokes' unusual name for the Emelius Arm in Charles Sound. Continuing the association to the names of their respective wives, Stokes named Fanny Island in Gold Arm after his wife and Eleanor Island after the colonel's wife, Eleanor Geddes.

Rocky Islet in Gold Arm. Black oystercatchers with chicks. (*J. Hall-Jones*)

Sunlit foot of "Merlin's Magic". (*J. Hall-Jones*)

"Merlin's Magic" appearing through the trees. (*J. Hall-Jones*)

Navigating the Irene River

For our first night in Charles Sound, Dieter and I camped amid the pretty, wooded islets of picturesque Gold Arm and watched the sun setting on the snow cone of Coronation Peak, standing high on the horizon. The next day we set out for Emelius Arm in high hopes of navigating the large Irene River, an ultimate experience for any kayaker. After negotiating the bar at the mouth we paddled up the deep, dark Irene River with its moss-laden boughs overhanging the peat-stained water. Here was the deepest silence and solitude which affected us both and we just drifted along without a word. We were equally moved by our sighting of the Marjorie Falls, which reveal themselves mysteriously through the trees on a side channel of the main river. No one knows who Marjorie was and how more appropriate is Lance Shaw's name "Merlin's Magic" for these mystically beautiful falls.

About five kilometres up the Irene River we were stopped by rapids. So we drifted quietly downriver to paddle around the lagoons at its mouth and camp for the night on the beach. From the bay we could see the great square summit of Mt Irene away at the head of the Irene Valley.

The Hinterland Explored

The strikingly square-shaped Mt Irene, the highest mountain in Western Fiordland, was an obvious distant fix for T. W. ("Tom") Preston's survey of Northern Fiordland in 1927. Although not approached by his party, it was named by one of his surveyors, Harold Smith ("Smithy"), after his wife Irene. The large Irene River which drains the western slopes of the massive mountain

Reflections in the still water of Irene River. (*J. Hall-Jones*)

was named much later by a Canterbury Museum expedition.

During the early 1950s the whole Mt Irene-Coronation Peak area was explored and mapped by Canterbury Museum expeditions of which I was fortunate enough to be a member. It was a great time to be around for those were the days before helicopters and topographical maps. The whole area was a huge blank space on the map labelled "unexplored".

The large Irene River Valley was still to be discovered, let alone mapped. Whereas today the easy approach to the hinterland would have been up this wide valley from Emelius Arm, in those days ready access from the sea was difficult and expensive to arrange. Instead, our expeditions set out from Te Anau by launch to be dropped off at the head of the South Fiord of Lake Te Anau. We then had to find a route through the unmapped rugged mountains to the plateau between Mt Irene and Coronation Peak. Our leader, Baughan Wisely, describes the discovery of unknown Coronation Peak graphically: "As we climbed up to the saddle [Te Au Saddle] the top of a new peak began to loom up in the U of the saddle like a mighty foresight of a gun; a most impressive and exciting experience." In those days we were all Empire loyalists and it being the Coronation of Queen Elizabeth II (1953) there was no question about it and we named the new peak Coronation. Nowadays the discoverers would probably have called it Republic Peak!

First Ascents of Mt Irene and Coronation Peak

On 27 January 1953 Baughan Wisely, ranger Phil Dorizac and the well-known photographer Robin Francis Smith began the first ascent of Mt Irene from Robin Saddle (named after the latter). "Our route led across a glacier", recounts Wisely, "and before we set off there was some discussion about this, for we were not equipped for alpine work having neither an ice-axe nor a rope between us. The first 100 feet across the hard, smooth ice was very awkward, as I was [only wearing] ankle

Below: Canterbury Museum expedition departing from Te Anau for the South Fiord. From left, front row: Ralph Wheeler, Baughan and Val Wisely, Alistair Carey. Second row: Burton Collins, the author, Tom Couzens, Jonathan Carey, passenger. (*R.F. Smith*).

Left: Coronation Peak from Te Au Saddle. Shangri-la Valley below. (*J. Hall-Jones*)

gumboots and on the verge of an acrobatic dance several times!" Fortunately the surface became softer and they gained the north ridge to the summit. Entering a couloir they "moved singly while the other two took shelter from the terrific showers of flying rocks". Eventually they wriggled out onto the summit to obtain a magnificent view of a frozen ocean of mountains as far north as Milford Sound. "We were looking at country, unexplored, unmapped and unknown", records Wisely. Dorizac spent two hours taking bearings to produce an accurate sketch map of the area, with a number of new names including Robin Saddle, Robin River (renamed Irene River), Coronation Peak and Lake Wisely.

The first attempt to climb Coronation Peak was in 1955, from our base camp on the Irene River plateau and up the northern ridge. Our party of seven was totally unequipped for climbing and we were unroped, which proved to be fortuitous as events turned out. As we entered a narrow and very steep rock gut Baughan Wisely was out in the lead. Suddenly we heard the ominous roar of a rock avalanche above us. Unfettered by a rope the six of us dived for the sides of the chimney, hugging the rock walls as closely as rocks have ever been hugged! As I crouched under a small ledge it

Mt Irene from our base camp. Irene River Valley, below left. (*J. Hall-Jones*)

received the full onslaught of the rocks, one of which bounced onto Jonathan Carey's forehead, splitting it open and mildly concussing him. As the roar and the dust subsided there was an awful silence, then whitened faces reappeared and voices were heard again. Thankfully, apart from Jonathan's injury, no one had been killed or maimed. The avalanche left us all a bit shaken, but after a 'breather' we climbed out of the gut only to be faced with an impossible vertical cliff on the north wall of the peak.

Frustrated by our failure, we then tried an eastern approach to the peak and in doing so we discovered a beautiful, secluded valley at the head of the Cozette Burn. With a succession of three hanging valleys and a waterfall from a lake at its head, it begged the name Shangri-la. But as yet this name has not been recognised by the New Zealand Geographic Board. Although the waterfall barred any approach to Coronation Peak from this side, we descended into Shangri-la Valley where amongst the snowgrass we found the typical straw droppings of notornis.

Coronation Peak was eventually climbed on 14 January 1955, by Baughan Wisely, Alistair Carey and Tom Couzens from the Irene Pass, by crossing its western icefield and ascending the south-east ridge. After admiring the magnificent views looking down on Charles, Nancy and Bradshaw Sounds, the climbers recorded their names and date on a piece of paper and placing it in a canister buried it under a cairn of rocks on the summit. Only recently the canister was found by a subsequent climber, but by then the lettering on the paper had become too faded to read.

Writing up the scientific finds of the expedition, geographer Ralph Wheeler recorded the Geiger radiation counts of the two geologists (Professor Douglas Coombs and Burton Collins) of 50 per minute, which was just below the lower limit of uranium, an element that they were searching for. On the ornithological side one party discovered a dead kakapo, about two months deceased.

In recognition of the Canterbury Museum expeditions' work in exploring and mapping this whole region, the New Zealand Geographic Board gave the name Museum Range to the mountains around Coronation Peak.

Members of the 1954-55 Canterbury Museum expedition on their return to the South Fiord. From left: Jonathan Carey, geologist Burton Collins celebrating with a cigar and bottle of whisky, John Hall-Jones in 'white' shorts, geographer Ralph Wheeler. (*Prof. D. Coombs*)

CHAPTER 12

Cruising the West Coast Fjords

The scenery is quite equal to the finest in the Alps, except in [the fjords] access is made easy by the incursion of the sea.
Sir James Hector, 1863

The little schooner *Matilda Hayes* (Captain John Falconer) was the first vessel on record to take passengers on a cruise of the magnificent West Coast Fjords. Knowing that winter was the best time to venture on the stormy West Coast, Captain Falconer sailed from Dunedin in May 1863 with Dr James Hector and the botanist-artist John Buchanan on board. But even in winter time the voyage was not without its hazards and we have seen how Hector

Painting from the head of Milford Sound by John Buchanan, botanist-artist aboard the *Matilda Hayes* in 1863. (*Hocken Library*)

Captain John Bollons of *ss Tutanekai*. (*E.R. Martin*)

dislocated his shoulder in Chalky Inlet and how the *Matilda Hayes* was frozen in at Doubtful Sound.

Approaching Milford Sound at dawn Dr Hector leaves us a graphic account of their entry into this majestic fjord. "The sharp serrated crests" of the summits appeared to form a "dark wall rising close to the water's edge. Then as the sun rose it slowly lit up the mountains in their true grandeur." As they proceeded up the fjord it became "contracted to a width of half a mile [at the Narrows] where its sides rise perpendicularly from the water's edge to 2,000 feet. The scenery is quite equal to the finest that can be enjoyed by the most difficult journeys into the Alps of the interior, except in this case access is made easy by the incursion of the sea into the alpine solitudes." From Milford Sound the *Matilda Hayes* continued to Martins Bay where Hector, guided by Henry Paramatta, walked through to Queenstown and back, then the *Matilda Hayes* returned down the Fiordland coast to Dunedin.

Governors Visit the Fjords

A cruise of the West Coast Fjords became a popular routine among the early Governors of New Zealand. The first in line was Sir George Bowen whose voyage in *HMS Clio* in 1871 almost ended disastrously when the ship struck the Clio Rock in Bligh Sound. Next came Sir James Fergusson in 1874, also in a Royal Navy ship *HMS Blanche*. The *Blanche's* name is displayed prominently among a list of 'visiting cards' nailed to a tree at Cemetery Point in Milford Sound.

By 1876 the government steamer *Hinemoa*, built specially for the purpose, was available to take Governors on these vice-regal cruises of the fjords. On 5 May 1877 the *Hinemoa* called at Milford Sound with the current Governor Lord Normanby on board. Governor Sir William Jervois apparently enjoyed these cruises so much that he visited Milford Sound twice in the *Hinemoa* in 1884 and 1888. On this second occasion Lady Jervois wrote a letter of apology to Donald Sutherland, who was away, explaining how she had borrowed some tea from his store for a picnic, but afterwards repaid it fourfold with 'Hinemoa' tea.

When it came to Governor Lord Ranfurly's 'turn' to visit the fjords in 1898 he wasn't quite so lucky. Originally Lord Ranfurly had expressed a wish to visit New Zealand's Subantarctic Islands when the government steamer *Tutanekai* (Captain John Bollons) next serviced the castaway depots there. This was duly approved and His Excellency was conducted on a cruise of the islands. But when he arrived back in Bluff he directed Captain Bollons to also visit the West Coast Fjords. As Captain Bollons endeavoured to explain to the Governor, the *Tutanekai* was already behind in its prime function of servicing the lighthouses with stores and this must take precedence over an unscheduled pleasure trip to the West Coast Fjords. Unable to reason with the Governor, Captain Bollons sent a telegram to his Minister of Marine, William Hall-Jones (later Sir William), who backed his captain to the ultimate extreme of threatening his resignation if the Governor got his way. Faced with a resolute Minister of the Crown, His Excellency really had no alternative but to disembark from the *Tutanekai,* albeit with some

Right: 'Visiting cards' of early cruise ships nailed to a tree at Cemetery Point, Milford Sound. (*J. H. Richards*)

The government steamer *Hinemoa* which conducted a number of Governors around the West Coast Fjords, but was also used twice as a prison ship. (*Alexander Turnbull Library*)

muttering about being "put off 'his' steamer". Captain Bollons was then able to get on with his real work of providing provisions to the needy lighthouse keepers, who were by then running short of food.

A Prison Ship

The *ss Hinemoa* was built in Scotland in 1876 at the same time as her sister-ship *ss Stella* but, as we have seen, the *Hinemoa* was specially designed as a government yacht. With white upper works, a yellow funnel and a bust of a Maori maiden mounted on her clipper bow, she was certainly a very handsome ship. But the *Hinemoa* was not always conducting Governors around the fjords.

On 14 December 1890 the *Hinemoa* arrived at Milford Sound with the Inspector General of Prisons, Alexander Hume, six prison officers and 45 prisoners to establish "Humeville Prison" at Sandfly Point, the start of the Milford Track. The prison camp would serve as a base to construct the track to Lake Te Anau, Hume wrote optimistically in Donald Sutherland's visitors book.

Two years later, with only two kilometres of track constructed by the prisoners, it was realised that the experiment of sending prison gangs to work in remote places was an expensive failure. On 24 August 1892 the *Hinemoa* arrived at Milford to re-embark the prisoners and return them to prison in Wellington. Donald Sutherland wrote in his visitors book: "The 40 thieves left for Wellington. A good thing for the Country that they have cleared out of this sound. Have no wish to see them again."

In 1889 the *Hinemoa* took over the job of servicing the lighthouses from her sister-ship the *Stella*, which was decommissioned from government service. In 1896 the *Tutanekai* replaced the *Hinemoa* and conducted the current Governor, the Earl of Glasgow, on a cruise of the West Coast Fjords. But, as we have seen, his successor Lord Ranfurly wasn't quite so lucky!

First Cruise Ship from Overseas

On 2 February 1874 the *ss Otago* (Captain J. McLean) on a cruise from Melbourne to Dunedin entered Milford Sound on the way – the first overseas passenger ship to do so. Her–'entry' "Otago 2/2/1874" takes pride of first place among the list of 'visiting cards' nailed to the tree at Cemetery Point.

In 1876 the *Otago* (Captain George Calder) was back again, this time with some distinguished passengers including Judge Stow of South Australia, the talented German artist Eugene von Guerard (then curator of the Melbourne Art Gallery) and some English tourists. The cruise had been advertised extensively in Melbourne and after four and a half days voyage, the *Otago* "entered the granite gates of Milford Sound at sunrise".

"Recent heavy rains caused one hundred waterfalls to flash and foam down the perpendicular mountains which enclose the inlet", wrote the newspaper reporter aboard the *Otago*. "The sun-tinted morning mists produced a spectacle of natural magic which the fortunate excursionists had never previously witnessed. The steamer anchored at the head of the Sound, close to the great Bowen Waterfall, at seven [a.m.] and remained there until noon next day.

Mr Eugene von Guerard at once had himself conveyed to [the beach in front of the present hotel] which with his rapid artistic instinct he had promptly fixed as the point of vision for his forthcoming [painting]. Here he remained all day making his pencil sketches."

The sketches included the *ss Otago* anchored in Freshwater Basin. Guerard's eventual painting in oil was on the grandest of scales, worthy of the grandeur of Milford Sound and caused a sensation when it was exhibited in Melbourne in 1877. A copy of this magnificent painting was chosen for the cover of the author's previous book *Milford Sound* and an enlarged portion is now reproduced, showing the artist wading ashore to make his preliminary sketches.

During the evening Captain Calder "illuminated the locality with a few rockets and blue lights and fired off the *Otago*'s [guns], arousing echoes which reverberated like long-continued thunder. Everyone was delighted, except perhaps the birds which mistook the blue lights for an unexpected morning sun and began flying about in an aimless, irrational way."

Regular Summer Cruises

On 19 January 1877 the Union Steamship Co.'s steamer *Wanaka,* with berths for 105 passengers, sailed from Port Chalmers on an excursion to the West Coast Fjords. Special amenities for the cruise included a piano, two large tubs for saltwater bathing and a cow to supply fresh milk! The voyage proved so popular that the company decided to make summer excursions an annual event.

The demand continued and six years later, when the much larger *ss Tarawera* was built, she took over the *Wanaka*'s summer schedule of cruising the fjords. The *Tarawera* (2,003 tons) was four times the tonnage of the *Wanaka* and had berths for 294 passengers. On her first excursion the *Tarawera* (Captain Cameron) sailed from Port Chalmers on 7 February 1883, entering Preservation and Chalky Inlets where she spent a night in each. Proceeding up the West Coast she visited all the other fjords, excluding Dagg, Nancy, Charles and Sutherland Sounds, before finally reaching Milford Sound.

On this maiden cruise of the fjords the *Tarawera*'s passengers included Sir James Hector and Sir Julius von Haast as lecturers and we have mentioned already how the two eminent geologists gave a discouraging opinion on the prospects of the Caswell Sound marble mine. Another passenger recounts how "almost everyone signed a requisition to Captain Cameron asking him to visit Hall Arm in Doubtful Sound, even if this meant missing some of the other

Eugene von Guerard's sketch of *ss Otago* anchored near the Bowen Falls, 1876. (*Alexander Turnbull Library*)

Eugene von Guerard's preliminary sketch from the head of Milford Sound, 24 January 1876. (*Alexander Turnbull Library*)

sounds, but not Milford". The petitioners got their wish and the *Tarawera* steamed all the way to the head of Doubtful Sound to reward them with the superb view of Mts Danae and Crowfoot through The Narrows of Hall Arm and the great bulk of Commander Peak at the entrance.

Anchoring at the head of Caswell Sound, "the boats, as usual, were soon out in all directions with the passengers fishing, shooting, sketching or just loafing. Some went up the river [Stillwater] in spite of the sandflies and after a while you could see the smoke of the various picnic parties curling up from the bush. As evening closed the various boats returned richly laden with ferns and trophies from the woods and the main deck looked like a market of plants with everyone busy boxing their spoils." (Obviously before Fiordland became a National Park!)

Proceeding to the head of George Sound they anchored near the magnificent Alice Falls, where some of the passengers scrambled up the dry gully alongside the waterfall to see Lake Alice at its head.

After the climax of their voyage at Milford Sound the *Tarawera* returned down the Fiordland coast, arriving back at Port Chalmers on 17 February, ten days after she set out. The excursion proved so successful that the *Tarawera* increased the number of cruises to two and even three each summer season, right

Left: From Eugene von Guerard's oil painting of Milford Sound, showing the artist wading ashore with his easel to sketch the scene. (*Art Gallery of N.S.W.*)

ss *Wanaka* which initiated the Union Steamship Company's regular summer cruises of the West Coast Fjords in 1877. (*Hocken Library*).

ss *Tarawera* anchored in Cuttle Cove, Preservation Inlet, while cruising the West Coast Fjords. (*Muir & Moodie*)

Picnicking on a tidal rock in Hall Arm, Mt Danae in background. *(J. Hall-Jones)*

up till 1897 when she was replaced by the *Waikare*.

With the development of the Milford Track the *Tarawera* usually stayed two nights in Milford Sound, allowing passengers to make an overnight trip to the Sutherland Falls. Chief Surveyor Charles Adams describes the *Tarawera*'s entrance into Milford Sound on one such excursion in 1892:

"The entrance to Milford Sound is so narrow that if the weather is at all thick it is very difficult to find it. As we proceed up the narrow passage the almost perpendicular mountains on either side seem to close in before us more and more, till it is difficult to believe there is a passage between them. The black walls of rock produce a feeling which is [almost] oppressive. Presently the passage opens a little, and we behold a most beautiful fall on our left [Stirling Falls]. The steamer keeps on her course leaving the Stirling Falls behind. Then the gun is fired, partly to apprise those [Donald Sutherland] at the head of the sound that we are coming and partly to give the passengers an opportunity of hearing the long reverberations that follow the report of the explosions. There in the distance are the Bowen

distinctive steam whistle which emitted "a wild, weird shriek" more like a siren than the conventional steamer's whistle.

Waikare Wrecked

In 1898 the company's new and larger ship *Waikare* (3,000 tons) replaced the *Tarawera* for the summer cruises of the West Coast Fjords. With berths for 214 first-class and 112 second-class passengers she was able to convey even

Left: Passengers from ss *Tarawera* boating in Wet Jacket Arm, Dusky Sound. *Tarawera* in background. (*F. Coxhead*)

Below: Boating party at the mouth of the Katherine River, George Sound. Alice Falls in background. (*F. Coxhead*)

Falls, at first view disappointing, but as we [draw] right abreast of them their full glory bursts upon us. While we are admiring their many beauties the sailors are busy mooring the ship to the red buoy at the head of the harbour and a boat is seen putting off from Sutherland's little jetty to welcome us. The steam launch is quickly crowded with those who have decided to make the excursion to the Sutherland Falls, while other remain behind sketching, photographing or just picnicking."

The journalist-climber Malcolm Ross was a passenger on the *Tarawera*'s last cruise of the fjords in 1897. He records that a regatta was held in George Sound, including a ladies' race in specially built boats and that a regatta ball was held in the evening, with the presentation of prizes to the winners of the boat races. On entering Milford Sound the *Tarawera* sounded its

Donald Sutherland (holding boat pole) meeting passengers from *ss Tarawera* at the head of Milford Sound. (*Hocken Library*)

Excursionists to the Sutherland Falls being landed at the start of the Milford Track. Steam pinnace from *Tarawera* anchored in Arthur River. (*Hocken Library*)

more tourists to the fjords. The *Waikare* continued these popular cruises right up till 1910, when she struck an uncharted rock in Dusky Sound. First Officer (later Captain) Gerald Doorly recounts:-

"After breakfast (on 4 January 1910) at our anchorage at Supper Cove we got under way and steamed down the sound at our full speed of 14 knots. In an hour's time the first glimpse of the ocean could be seen between the islands guarding the entrance to the inlet. All boats had been snugly stowed and secured and the stewards were preparing the meal tables for lunch.

But as the ship was passing between Indian Island on the left, and Passage Islets on the right – a channel half a mile wide – a terrific crash shook the ship from stem to stern, then another crash and bang, followed by another which lifted the stern almost out of the water. There was no doubt what had happened – we had struck and bumped over an uncharted rock!

'ALL HANDS ON DECK!' The carpenter rushed out with his sounding rod and quickly sounded the bilges, while the crew hurried along and clambered up ladders to their boat stations. Tearing up on to the bridge I found the captain (W. J. Newton), pale-faced but perfectly calm, examining the chart.

'There's no rock here!' he said. 'The soundings show no bottom at 132 fathoms!'

Almost immediately the ship listed heavily over to starboard. 'Clear away and lower the boats!' ordered the captain, at the same time giving the company's signal of two blasts on the steam whistle. It certainly looked as if the vessel was about to founder in the deep water. Could we run the ship ashore? No likely places seemed to be near at hand – all around us were precipitous islands with apparently deep water up to their shores.

The chief engineer arrived on the bridge and reported that part of the engine-room floor-bed had been raised about a foot. Water was pouring into the stokehold and engine-room, and had already reached the lower furnaces. He might be able to keep the engines going for five minutes – with luck! The Captain decided to try and make for Stop Island, about one mile away, close to which the chart showed a low rocky ledge with soundings of nine to twelve fathoms.

By this time the boats were in the water and lifebelts served out to everybody. The passengers behaved with great coolness, and many of the women discarded their skirts in the event of having to make boats, and were all away from the ship's side fifteen minutes after striking the rock.

It was imperative to stop the engines because of the danger of the propeller hitting any of the boats as they drifted astern. The fine work performed by the engineers and stokehold hands must not be forgotten. Within two minutes of the vessel's striking, every pump was going full bore and the watertight doors closed. One does not need much imagination to picture the situation below, with the water rushing in under the boilers and engines until the men were up to their breasts in water.

The boats followed the ship, which moved ahead slowly by fits and starts, the captain steering her to her final resting place. 'Finished-with-engines!' crashed in the bridge telegraph from the engine-room before Stop Island was reached, but happily the way on the ship carried her to shore.

Her bows rumbled on to the rocks, and I remember the lively capers the carpenter and I performed dodging the branches of the trees as the forecastle became buried in the overhanging bush. We dropped the anchors into the dense scrub, and fortunately the fore part of the ship remained stationary. Lines were then run from the stern and made fast to

trees to keep the ship from swinging off the shore. On grounding she stood upright for a few moments then fell over to port with a sickening jerk.

The passengers having landed on the rocky 'beach', the boats returned to the ship, into which we dumped the luggage – laboriously hove up by hand from the hold – provisions, water casks, mattresses, bedding, hatches, etc. All awnings and spars, too, were slashed down and boated ashore. Even the ship's piano was taken ashore. Then the carpenter, with gangs of sailors and passengers, set about finding a suitable site for a camp. After beating a track through the dense bush they reached some sort of clearing at the top of the island – about 100 feet up from the rocks – and the awnings were dragged up the slope and spread over tree trunks sawn off at a convenient height.

Before dark the camp was occupied, and any loose gear stacked safely in the bush above high-water mark. For a finishing touch all the hurricane lamps were hung about on trees and these, together with the cooking fires, cast a weird glow on the surroundings. The firelight attracted to the scene an occasional weka whose inquisitiveness brought forth startled shrieks from different parts of the camp during the night. Water rats, too, paid us unwelcome visits."

All 141 passengers and 85 crew had been landed safely on Stop Island. As it appeared likely that relief would not be forthcoming for a day or two, all the unmarried young ladies and a stewardess were transferred by launch to Richard Henry's hut, then unoccupied. "In no time they had the rooms swept out, beds made up, kindling chopped, the stove going and wild flowers arranged in empty jam jars".

Meantime Second Officer Appleyard had set out in the "oil launch" for the Puysegur

Above left: Some of the passengers and crew of the *Waikare* photographed shortly after the holed ship was beached on Stop Island. (*Otago Witness*)

Left: The unmarried young ladies being transferred by launch to Richard Henry's hut on Pigeon Island. (*Otago Witness*)

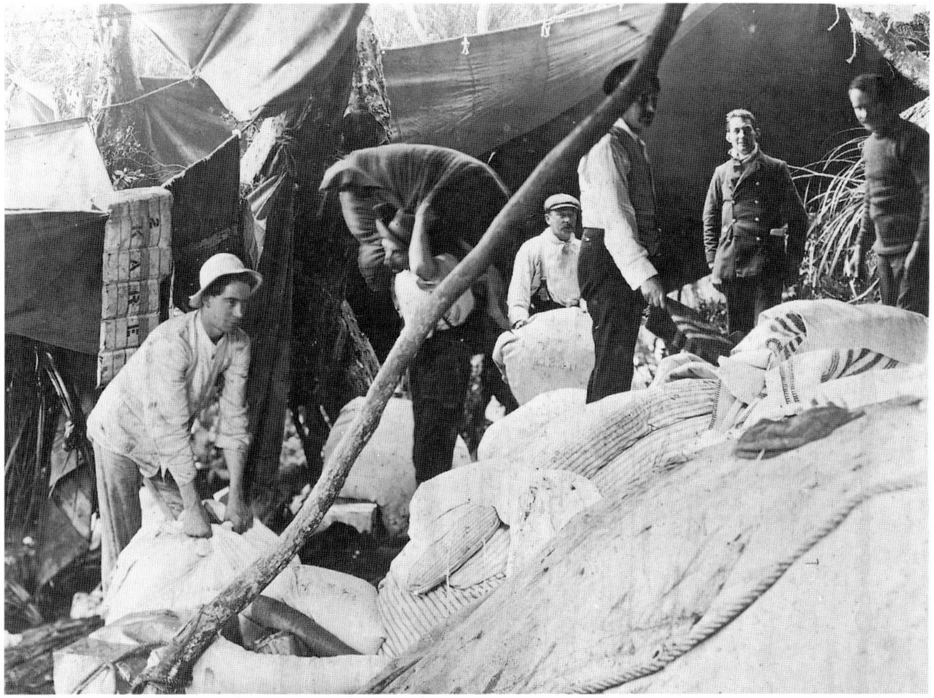

Setting up camp on Stop Island. (*Southland Museum*)

Point Lighthouse (40 kilometres away), where he arrived on the same day as the wreck to send a telegram out asking for help. Appleyard returned to Stop Island on the following day (5 January) bearing a telegram reply that a rescue steamer was leaving Port Chalmers for Dusky Sound.

You can imagine the surprise and joy of the castaways (a total of 226 souls) when a man-o'-war came steaming into the Sound that same afternoon. The stranded passengers had been doubly lucky. The warship *HMS Pioneer* (Commander Blunt) just happened to be bunkering in the nearer port of Bluff at the time and the Prime Minister (the local M.P. Sir Joseph Ward) just happened to be visiting Invercargill. Learning of the disaster, Ward ordered Commander Blunt to proceed to the rescue at all possible speed.

Happily, by 6 p.m. that evening all the passengers had been transferred to *HMS Pioneer,* but a dozen of the crew, including Captain Newton, remained behind on Stop Island in the hope of salvaging the *Waikare*. "Dirty, sore and tired, we slept like logs until midnight", records Doorly, "when the carpenter aroused us with a cry: 'She's going! God sir, she's going!' Poor 'Chips' had witnessed the birth of the old ship at Dumbarton and had lived intimately with her ever since; her death struggle was wringing the soul casing out of him."

"Peering through the trees we could see the dim outline of the dying vessel ... Presently the stillness was broken by a rattle of cable chains and with a dull, grinding sound, the ship slid astern and rumbled heavily over to port, accompanied by a ghastly crashing and smashing: the funnel toppled, and the foremast met the water with a great splash and disappeared. The bow rose and water gushed from the fatal jagged holes as it lay, a sheer hulk, sideways on the rocks while the stern was swallowed up greedily in the inky depths. Eerie moans and gurgles escaped from the air vents, and the displaced waters swished about uncannily among the rocks. Then the crescent moon peeped out from behind the lowering clouds, and an intense silence settled upon the face of the dark waters. The end of the *Waikare* – her commission was over .... 'Chips' grasped my hand. He couldn't speak. He was crying."

Passengers fishing while they wait to be rescued. The wrecked *Waikare* still held by mooring lines to Stop Island. (*I. D. Williams*)

The next day the *ss Moura* Captain McDonald arrived and the 'death watch' transferred all the salvaged gear and boats to the *Moura*. "Thoroughly worn out we flung ourselves down on the deck and as the ship steamed away we gazed to the last, sadly, at the capsized bows – all that remained visible of our late floating home."

At the subsequent Court of Inquiry Captain Newton was exonerated from all blame and indeed was praised for the prompt action he took after the *Waikare* struck the uncharted rock and for the able manner in which he tended to the needs and comfort of all those under his care. As Captain Newton left the Court he received a telegram from his wife: "Cheer up. Come home. We can always keep fowls. Love."

The capsized *Waikare* soon slid off the rock shelf and sank into the depths. Over the years many 'bits and pieces' from the wreck have been salvaged by divers and some of these can be seen on display at the Te Anau DOC museum.

Cruise Ships Return

The loss of the *Waikare* put an abrupt stop to cruises of the West Coast Fjords for almost two decades. Then, in 1928, D. McKay Ltd of Invercargill laid on a fjords' cruise in the wooden steamer

Left: Captain Newton (on right) departing from Stop Island with Captain McDonald of the *Moura*. (*Otago Witness*)

Above right: Russell Duncan's party standing on the capsized hull of the *Waikare* shortly after she was wrecked. (*Photograph Russell Duncan, 1910. Courtesy Mrs Janet Menzies*)

Right: HMS Pioneer arriving unexpectedly only one day after the wreck. (*I. D. Williams*)

Tent and galley where the *Waikare* salvage party lived until rescued by the *Moura*. (*Photograph by Russell Duncan, 1910. Courtesy Mrs Janet Menzies.*)

Right: Cruise ship *Monowai* anchored in Harrison Cove, Milford Sound, 1933. Glaciated Mt Pembroke on left. (*J. Churchouse*)

Kotare. The *Kotare* proceeded directly from Bluff to Milford Sound with "over 30 passengers" and spent several days there. Plucking up courage she returned via the fjords and entered Dusky Sound, the *Waikare*'s last resting place.

The trip was a great success and McKay decided to purchase the old government steamer *Hinemoa* for further cruises. Described as "the most graceful steamer afloat", the *Hinemoa* offered eight-day cruises of the fjords for a total cost of "16 guineas, with 2 guineas extra for the use of the [old vice-regal] state-room". They must have been idyllic days, sailing in the old vice-regal yacht, with frequent shore excursions and bountiful returns from fishing expeditions. But the Depression brought an end to such luxury cruises and in 1932 the *Hinemoa* was laid up.

Paradoxically the Depression brought more, larger cruise ships into Milford Sound, with companies seeking employment for their out-of-work liners. One of them was the Union Steamship Co.'s *ss Monowai*, which made her first visit to the Sound in 1933. Many years later, in 1994, she returned to the West Coast Fjords as *HMNZS Monowai* to revise the *Acheron* chart of 1851. Another liner *ss Wanganella* also visited Milford Sound in 1933, on her maiden voyage across the Tasman Sea. Later, as we have seen, she ended her days as a floating hostel for the power scheme workers at Deep Cove.

After the Second World War few vessels could be spared for cruising. Appropriately their return to the fjords was heralded by the Royal Yacht *Gothic,* which entered Milford Sound in 1954 with Queen Elizabeth and the

Duke of Edinburgh on board. In 1978 Her Majesty's namesake, the liner Queen Elizabeth II, visited Milford Sound. Hundreds of tourists drove through to Milford to see the world's largest cruise ship amid the setting of some of the world's finest scenery. Other global liners followed and in recent years Milford Sound has been visited by a dozen or more cruise ships annually.

Nature Cruises

In a more modest but more companionable way, two companies offer regular cruises of the fjords, mostly in the winter time when the weather is more settled and the sandflies are at their minimum. The Fiordland Travel Co.'s scow *Milford Wanderer* runs a seven day cruise of Doubtful Sound, Dusky Sound, Preservation and Chalky Inlets, with historian and nature lecturer-guides and plenty of trips ashore. Likewise, Lance Shaw's yacht *Breaksea Girl* visits these southern fjords, also the northern fjords right up to Milford Sound. Other vessels are available for nature tours on a charter basis.

Milford Wanderer in Crooked Arm, Doubtful Sound. (*J. Hall-Jones*)

Left: Huge overseas liner *Rotterdam* (38,000 tons) anchored in Harrison Cove. (*C. Howell*)

Facing page, left: Waterfall in Acheron Passage framed in the rigging of the *Milford Wanderer*. (*J. Hall-Jones*)

Facing page, right: Lance Shaw's *Breaksea Girl* berthed at Deep Cove, Doubtful Sound. (*J. Hall-Jones*)

and an observation submarine offer the non-diver a glimpse of the beautiful underwater world of the fjords.

Whether you view them from above or below, the West Coast Fjords have a magnificence and majesty of their own. This vast wilderness of deep glacier-carved fjords, wooded islands and steep craggy mountains is preserved in perpetuity as a World Heritage Park.

Left: Eager seakayakers take to the sea in Milford Sound. (*J. Hall-Jones*)

Below: Lance Shaw examining a large tree of delicate black coral (*DOC*)

But if you really want to get close to nature, away from the noise and the crowd, seakayaking is the optimal way to go. To have dolphins porpoising in front of your bow, to have seals bobbing towards you, fearless in their curiosity, to sneak up close to a penguin quietly preening itself, or to kayak up a stillwater river with overhanging boughs – seakayaking in the fjords must surely be the ultimate wilderness experience.

The same can be said of the diver exploring the unseen depths of the fjords. Here in this underwater wonderland are quill-shaped sea pens, the only ones in New Zealand; up to four metre trees of black coral, the largest black coral population in the world; and brachiopods (lamp shells), living fossils which have been in existence for over 600 million years. To protect these unique inhabitants of the West Coast Fjords, marine reserves have been set aside in Doubtful and Milford Sounds. At the latter an underwater observatory

Bibliography

Adams, C. W. *The Great Sutherland Waterfall,* Tasmania, 1892.
Banwell, D. B. *Wapiti in New Zealand,* Reed, 1966.
Beaglehole, J. C. *The Journals of Captain James Cook,* Hakluyt Soc., 1955-67.
Beattie, J. H. *The Maoris of Fiordland,* Dunedin, 1949.
Far-famed Fiordland, Dunedin, 1950.
Begg, A. C. & N. C. *Dusky Bay,* Whitcombe & Tombs, 1966.a
Port Preservation, Whitcombe & Tombs, 1973.
The World of John Boultbee, Whitcoulls, 1979.
Calvert, R. *Te Mere O Tarawai,* 1994
Cox, J. H. *Mt Solitary Copper Lode,* Geological Survey Reports, 1877.
Crozier, A. *Beyond the Southern Lakes,* Reed, 1950.
Doorly, G. *In the Wake,* Melbourne.
Dorizac, P. *YMCA Adventure Camps,* 1966-67.
Duggan, B. *Incidental History,* Taradale, 1997.
Edge, D. *The Sounds of New Zealand,* Sea Breeze, 1994.
Forster, J. R. *The Resolution Journal of Johann Forster,* Hakluyt Soc., 1982.
Foster, P. *A Boaties' Guide to Fiordland,'*Mana Cruising Club, 1994.
Grange, K. *The Underwater World of Fiordland,* Forest & Bird, 1986.
Hall-Jones, F.G. *Sir William Hall-Jones,* Dunedin, 1969.
Hall-Jones, J. *Fiordland Explored,* Reed, 1976.
Fiordland Place-names, FNPB, 1979.
Goldfields of the South, Craigs, 1984.
Doubtfull Harbour, Craigs, 1997.
Discover Fiordland, Craigs, 1997.
Milford Sound, Craigs, 2000.
Hansard, G. *Journal of the Acheron*, Hocken Library, 1851.
Hector, J. *Geological Expedition West Coast,* Otago Prov. Gaz. 1863, p435.
Henry, R. *Habits of Flightless Birds of N.Z.,* Govt Printer, 1903.
Hill, S. & J. *Richard Henry of Resolution Island,* McIndoe, 1987.
Hislop, B. Unpublished letter, 1889.
Howard, G. *Power from Fiordland,* Education Dept, 1974.
Hunt, A.L. *Confessions of A. Leigh Hunt,* Reed, 1951.
Hutchins, L. *Making Waves,* Craigs, 1999.
McCraw, J. *Coastmaster,* Craigs, 1999.
McKay, A. *Recent Discoveries Milford Sound,* Trans. N.Z. Inst., 1883.
McKerrow, J. Survey Report, Otago Prov. Gaz. 1863, p351.
McLauchan, G. *The Line that Dared,* Dunedin, 1987.
McNab, R. *Murihiku and the Southern Islands,* Whitcombe & Tombs, 1907.
Martin, E.R. *Marine Department Centennial History*, Govt Printer, 1969.
Menzies, A. J. *Journal* in McNab's *Murihiku.*
Morrison, K. *Notes on the History of Doubtful Sound,* 1975.
Murry, R. *Journal* in McNab's *Murihiku.*
O'Hagan, S. *Report on Docherty's Mine,* 1976, D.OC. Te Anau.
Orchiston, J. *Exploration S.W. Otago 1896,* N.Z. Surveyor, 1928.
Paulin, R. *The Wild West Coast of New Zealand,* London, 1889.
Peat, N. & Patrick, B. *Wild Fiordland,* Dunedin, 1996.
Poole, A.L. *N.Z.-American Fiordland Expedition 1947*, Govt Printer, 1951.
Reischek, A. *Yesterdays in Maoriland,*—London, 1930.
Caesar: The Wonderful Dog, Auckland, 1939.
Richards, G. *New Zealand Pilot,* 1856.
Ross, J. O. *This Stern Coast,* Reed, 1969.
Ross, M. *The West Coast Sounds,* 1897.
Smith, I. & Gillies, K. *Archaeological Investigations at Luncheon Cove,* 1997, DOC.
Archaeological Investigations at Facile Harbour, 1998, DOC.
Smith, T. G. *Man the Light*, Auckland, 1996.
Sparrman, A. *A Voyage Round the World,* London, 1944.
Tustin, K. *A Wild Moose Chase,* Dunedin, 1998.
Wales, W. *Journal* in Beaglehole's *Journals of Captain Cook,* Vol. 2.
Wheeler, R. *Expedition into Fiordland,* N.Z. Geographer, 1955.
White, W. *Lore and History of South Island Maori,* Bascands, 1952.
Wisely, B. *Mt Irene and Fiordland Exploration,* N.Z. Alpine Journal, 1953.

Index

Text: 10/12 New Century Schoolbook
Paper: 128gsm silk matt art
Book jacket: 128gsm gloss art
Book design: Ellen van Empel
Book bound by S. I. McHarg Bookbinders, Christchurch, New Zealand.
Printed by Craig Printing Company Limited, Invercargill, New Zealand.

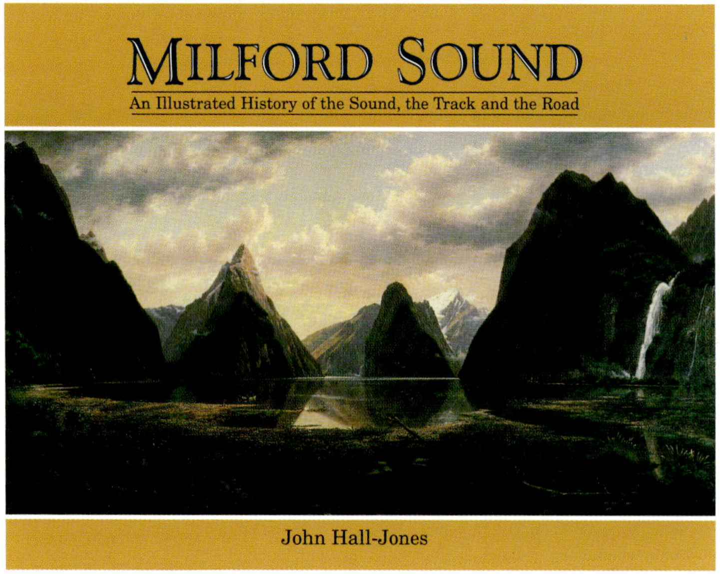

Now that you have read ***The Fjords of Fiordland*** you may wish to obtain a copy of its companion volume, ***Milford Sound.*** Described by one reviewer as "an enlightening journey to the Sound", the book enlarges on the early history of MILFORD SOUND and records the early history of the MILFORD TRACK and the MILFORD ROAD. There are also chapters on the pioneer township of Te Anau, the original steamers on Lake Te Anau and the students who cut the Grave-Talbot Track before the road went through.

The book contains an oustanding collection of 300 early photographs of the Sound, the Track and the Road – the great majority of which have never been published before.

Here are the stories of:

- the discovery of the Mackinnon Pass
- the epic task of constructing the Milford Road and Homer Tunnel
- the deeds of brave William Quill who climbed the Sutherland Falls
- Jim Dennistoun who made the first ascent of Mitre Peak in a pair of gym shoes!
- surveyor John Christie who descended the awful cliffs of the Homer Saddle on a wire rope.

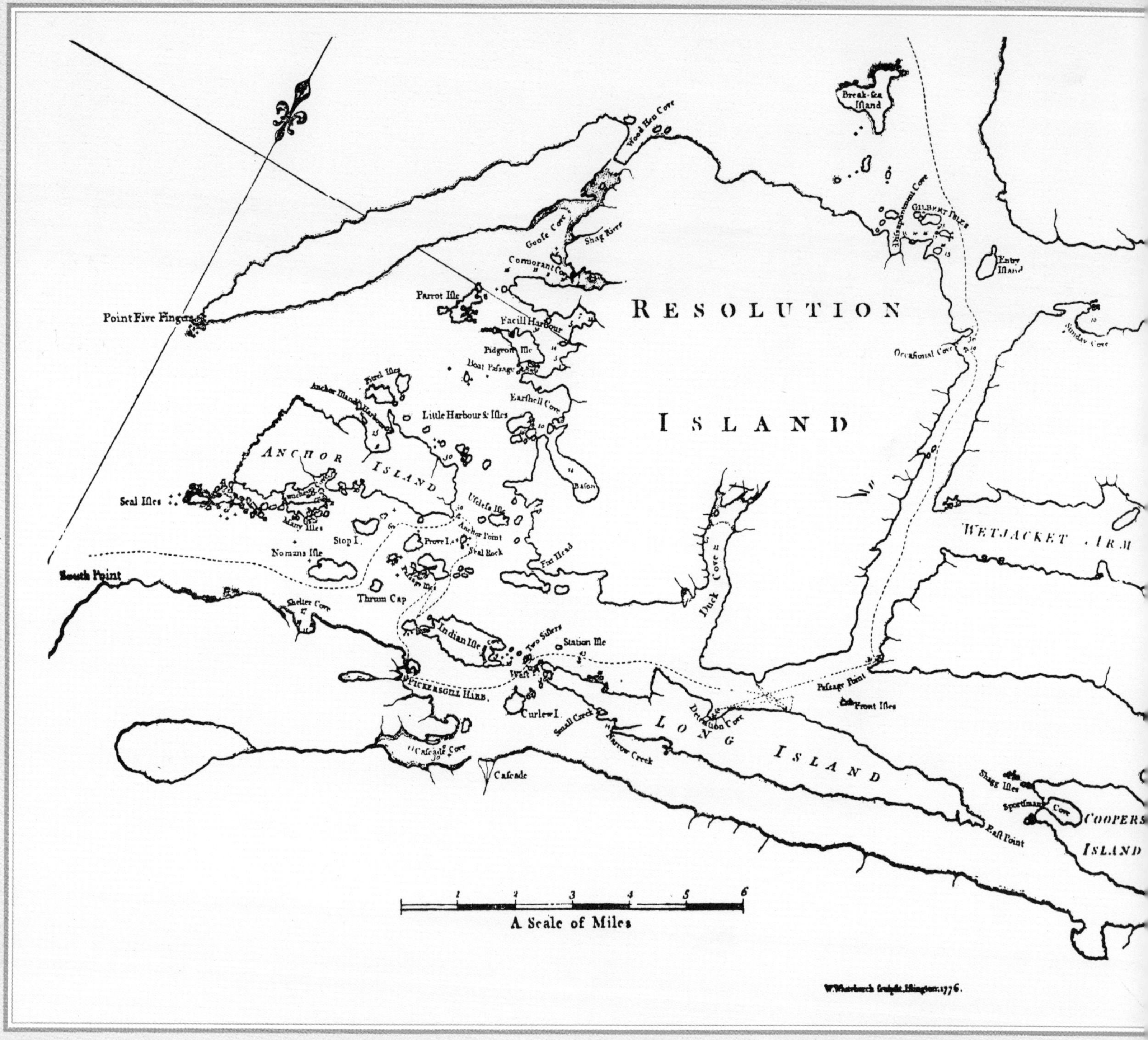

Captain James Cook's chart of "Dusky Bay", 1773. *(Admiralty)*